Old Alexandria

OLD
ALEXANDRIA
Where America's Past is Present

*Four walking tours through the lively Virginia
port, past its architecturally beautiful 18th
century houses, into churches and public buildings,
plus visits to archeological digs and the old
ramparts. With map and 66 photographs.*

Nettie Allen Voges

FOREWORD BY JAMES W. COLDSMITH, CHAIRMAN
ALEXANDRIA BICENTENNIAL COMMISSION

ORIGINAL PHOTOGRAPHS BY PATRICIA DALZELL

EPM PUBLICATIONS, INC.

Library of Congress Cataloging in Publication Data

Voges, Nettie Allen.
  Old Alexandria: where America's past is present

  Bibliography: p. 204.
  1. Alexandria, Va.—Description—Tours. 2. Historic
buildings—Virginia—Alexandria—Guide-books.
3. Alexandria, Va.—Buildings. I. Title.
F234.A3V63   917.55′296′044   75-23343
ISBN 0-914440-10-1

EPM Publications, Inc., 1003 Turkey Run Road, McLean, Va. 22101
Printed in the United States of America

Design by Anne Hanger
Typesetting by The Monotype Composition Co.

Cover photo: Re-enactment of an historic event in front of Gadsby's
Tavern. Reproduced courtesy of the Alexandria Tourist Council.

Frontispiece: Alexandria Lyceum, now serving as the George Washington
Northern Virginia Bicentennial Center.

To the memory
of Margaret Brent, 1600–1671
a gracious and enterprising Virginia Gentlewoman
in my family line

ACKNOWLEDGMENTS

I am profoundly grateful to all my predecessors who, in their time and style, with love for a gallant, endearing and historic port town in Virginia, have studied its records, listened to its legends, and written its history. From each I have learned much and from each I have acquired courage to write about Old Alexandria. Although I am not a native, my family roots are more than three centuries deep in the soil of Northern Virginia; and thirty years of preferential residence in Alexandria have given me opportunity to look into its heart, love its people, and catch a measure of its spirit.

I am grateful, also, to the old Moravian Church community of Salem, now a part of Winston-Salem, North Carolina. Here I was born and reared; and here I learned from the beginning that the past, with all those who created it, forms the tapestried backdrop against which the drama of the present is daily performed.

There is special indebtedness to many persons and organizations for aid and encouragement in the preparation of this book: James W. Coldsmith, chairman of the Bicentennial Commission, who so kindly provided the Foreword; Julie

Perry, director, and Commission members Emily S. Alexander, Walter V. Barbash, Philip C. Books, Mildred F. Councilor, Marion M. Duncan, Ruth L. Gaskins, Nancy G. Gilbert, Robert G. Lineberry, Orlando D. Martino, Elena H. Mattie, Harold G. Pollard, Elsa Rosenthal, Robert E. Shufflebeam, Thelma R. Wair, Monroe Whitton and Seymour Young, and to the entire staff of the Bicentennial Center; Peg Sinclair, director, Alexandria Tourist Council, and staff members Barbara Crews, Ruth Hubard and Catherine Lazarus; Margaret D. Calhoun, research director, Alexandria Library, and the library staff for assistance in locating and studying the extensive collection of *Alexandriana* maintained by the Library; Colonel Wilfred J. Smith, president, Alexandria Historical Society, and members of the executive committee for their encouragement at the outset of this project; Ethelyn Cox for advice at numerous points when documentation about buildings was required; Bert H. Davis, Watertown, N. Y., associate through most of my professional career, whose editorial assistance was invaluable; William Robert Adam, curator, Gadsby's Tavern, for photographs and information about restoration plans of the Tavern; Dorothy H. Kabler, for permission to use some of the material from her history of Gadsby's Tavern; Edith Pobst Peterson, regent, John Alexander Chapter, NSDAR, Lloyd Smoot Seaman and Elizabeth Sherier tenHouten for permission to study the manuscript files of the Chapter concerning John Alexander and the Alexander family; and to Ann Mays Andrews for additional assistance in locating information about early Indian inhabitants of Northern Virginia; John K. Pickens, chairman, Alexandria Archeological Commission, Richard Muzzrole, City Archeologist, and members of the Commission for assistance and photographs in preparing the section on this project; Elizabeth McIvor, of the City Hall staff, for cooperation in photographing the original minute book of the first Alexandria trustees; Marvin L. Fowler, William Adrian Brown and Edward Buckmaster, curators of the George

Washington National Memorial, for their courteous assistance in preparing the section on Enshrined Treasures; Esther Holliday Green and Donald C. Slaugh, for assistance in connection with the Stabler-Leadbeater Apothecary Shop; Gradie Philipp for information about the Keyes house; Marshall J. Beverley, former mayor of Alexandria, for information about the Friendship Veterans Fire Engine Company; the curators of the Fitzhugh-Lee and Lee-Fendall houses for photographs; Joseph Cipolari and Edward Plyler for permission to photograph the garden of the Edmund Jennings Lee House and Betty Wright for permission and assistance in photographing the kitchen of the Dr. William Brown House; Colonel Joseph Mitchell, curator, Fort Ward Park, for pictures and information about the Park; Frederick Tilp, for assistance in securing old photographs of the waterfront, Marlene Miller, Women's Editor, *The Gazette*, and to innumerable friends who listened patiently to my questions and provided answers.

I am also indebted to a succession of owners of all the private residences mentioned in this book who, during their time of ownership conducted research about individual buildings and shared it with me in connection with tours of old houses; and finally, to Dr. Laurence Adams Malone whose encouragement and companionship through the often musty morass of historic research added a dimension of delight to the preparation of this work.

Nettie Allen Voges

FOREWORD

Alexandria is a most unusual place. It has some very special buildings and sites that are visited each year by hundreds of thousands of people. What frustrates those of us who live and work here is that far too many of our visitors walk unseeingly or unknowingly past dozens of American historical architectural and cultural gems.

Alexandria surrounds you with literally thousands of tangible everyday realities from another age—the age that made us what we are. Here you stand at the real heart of the whole American experience. Everyone thrills at the marvelous diversity of America's people. But it was here that the men of the mainstream gathered 200 years ago. Their talk of politics and freedom at Gadsby's Tavern and at John Carlyle's house led not only to revolution and independence, but it defined most of the important freedoms we enjoy today as Americans.

One of the remarkable facts about Alexandria is that its citizens have managed to preserve so much and use it the way it was meant to be used. Here old houses remain houses, with people living in them. Christ Church and the Old Presbyterian Meeting House are still churches. John Gadsby's famous tavern is being made into a tavern again. Old seaport warehouses become import shops with regularity. Even the city's Bicentennial Center has an adaptive use from the original. It was built in 1839 by the Lyceum Company in cooperation with the Library Company. It was a library, a small museum, and a meeting hall cum social and intellectual center. And it remains a massively important example of Greek revival architecture.

Bicentennial comes as naturally to Alexandria as the brick sidewalks, cobblestones and the ancient boxwoods because there is so much to see here and so many of the basic roots of the American Revolution are deep in our soil. The Bicentennial activity in Alexandria is a result of the same sort of feeling that motivated the early patriots who lived here. It included citizens of all kinds, colors and ages.

A great many people will be very glad that Nettie Allen Voges was one who started thinking about the Bicentennial. I had known Mrs. Henry Voges before, but one day when we both had business in a printing shop in the Old Town, I had a chance to watch her deal with the problems of her project. There she was, sitting at a borrowed typewriter in a busy office dashing off the most delightful 18th Century prose I had ever read. From that moment I knew she was a special kind of writer. She can write anything any way it needs to be written.

There are two reasons we should be particularly happy she decided to do this Bicentennial edition about Alexandria. First, she understands the essence of old Alexandria. She knows its atmosphere is created by thousands and thousands of small and beautiful details. Second, she knows exactly where and what they mean. For years she has been absorbed in the detail of the city without losing sight of the whole. As a writer, she has been sharing that knowledge and understanding bit by bit in pieces she has done for forums, homes tours and anything else that was requested. But the idea that Nettie Allen Voges is now putting her perceptions into book length almost makes it worth waiting for the Bicentennial.

Alexandria is important in American history in terms of what was said here about freedom 200 years ago: the Fairfax Resolves, the Virginia Bill of Rights. Alexandria is important in terms of what it says about American freedom today. And this book is an important part of the message.

James W. Coldsmith, Chairman
Alexandria Bicentennial Commission

CONTENTS

13

Tour 3 HOUSES WITH A PAST AND A PRESENCE

An hour's walk through Old Town calling attention to many private residences with historic and architectural interests 129

Tour 4 OLD CHURCHES AND CEMETERIES 151

PART 3 ENSHRINED TREASURES

Visit to George Washington National Masonic Memorial; by car or bus, about one mile from Old Town, west on King Street. Open to public. Guided tours to parapet with 20-mile panoramic view in all directions. Replica of Alexandria-Washington Lodge No. 22 and George Washington Memorial Museum 165

PART 4 ALEXANDRIA DIGS UP ITS PAST

Information about archeological excavations and exploration underway in the old port section, the archeological laboratory and exhibits of restored artifacts 175

1   Where Past is Present

OLD ALEXANDRIA TODAY

ALEXANDRIA, VIRGINIA is different from most other old towns. Her perceptive visitors are quickly aware of an atmosphere that catches them up into the spirit of the old port section. There is life, activity, bustle here. There always has been.

Wherever you look, you see ancient buildings bearing markers attesting to their lineage, comfortably shouldered for the large part by architecturally congenial newer structures. And these have, themselves, taken on the flavor of the area. Market Square in Alexandria is still Market Square, the first of two lots set apart for specific purposes when the town was founded in 1749. The Square is larger today, more open, with comfortable benches for those wishing to enjoy the view. Gone for all time are a whipping post, the hitching rails, Sharpshin Alley and the rumbling of wagon traffic over the cobblestones. Yet two blocks of cobblestones do remain, so roughly contoured that present day traffic avoids them, thus providing a measure of privacy to the old houses that line the streets. An historic church-spire lifts eyes upward, but there are no obtruding glass-and-steel stalagmites to tower above

King Street today looking toward the river.

such streets as King and Queen, Prince and Princess, and Duke—without a Duchess.

The atmosphere is not contrived, not created by restored similarity to or approximation of the past; nor does it come strangering in from the river which eddies with easy familiarity at the foot of old streets. It is generated by a quality of natural vitality that belonged to Alexandria in the beginning and that springs freely from its founding sources. Alexandria, moving steadily into its third century of everyday living, is on its way.

The old part of the town is block after block after block of outwardly unpretentious small shops, straggling away now and then into stone-paved alleys, and offering an unbelievable selection of "things from everywhere," with not one neon sign to dim the silver sheen of night on the river. There are flower stalls and book marts, arcades that invite exploration through brick archways, handcrafts and workshops and studios and, of course, antiques. Old riverfront warehouses, converted to new uses, are crammed to the eaves with merchandise from ships that anchor nearby. And always proud, even a trifle boastful of its eating places, the old town has them: upstairs, downstairs, on the main streets, through the narrow alleys, whose specialties range from the Old Virginia favorites to a variety of international cuisines.

Old Alexandria is also formal eighteenth century houses whose doorways, dentiled cornices and mantels have won the admiration of many architects. It is rows of small houses, one a scant seven feet wide, toeing uneven brick sidewalks like the earnest young soldiers who drilled in the Square before following General Braddock into the "western wilderness." It is tantalizing glimpses through narrow gates into walled gardens, where no gardens are suspected, but where old boxwood is always fragrant and azaleas and camellias bloom in season. It is a fountain whose spray turns to spun gold in the morning sun. And it is a view, backward to "how it was" and forward to "how it will be."

Best of all, Alexandria offers an invitation to investigate. Here visitors can stroll comfortably, looking in and looking around, browsing and asking questions and recreating the old port. For the imaginative, there come clamor and color from commerce: pipe-clenching sea captains striding the streets, rope walks and sail lofts, ox-carts churning up mud, bank-bound Scottish merchants with their minds on business, and full-skirted matrons nimbly crossing the street on stepping stones. Here are strange ships tied up at the wharf and sailors swinging in and out of the riverside taverns. As a light breeze comes off the Potomac, there can be an awareness of the serenity born of age that invites reflection coupled with the curiosity of youth eager to look in just one more shop and frame for memory just one more picturesque doorway.

HISTORIC BACKGROUND, 1607 TO 1749

Alexandria came into existence as a town on a hot July morning in 1749* when the half-acre lots of a 60-acre tract lying within a curve of the Potomac River between two points of land which served as boundaries were put up for public auction.

The beginning of Alexandria is so closely related to the first permanent colonizing efforts of the English in America that a review of some high points in early American history may be helpful.

Sir Walter Raleigh faced his Queen Elizabeth on an his-

---

* The date given for the founding of Alexandria in old records, histories and on markers is July 13, 1749. This date is according to the old Julian calendar which was still in use at that time. In 1751, by royal decree, the Gregorian calendar was adopted as "the law of the land" for England and her colonies. September 2, 1751, officially became September 14, and thereafter, eleven days were added to "old style" dates to bring them into conformity. Thus, George Washington, born February 11, 1732 old style, was born on February 22 new style. The date of the founding of Alexandria is July 13, old style, and July 24 new style.

toric day. The explorer and adventurer came to present a large and pleasant portion of the New World to his monarch, who would thereafter consider it Crown property. He told Elizabeth that this goodly possession, occupied by the red-skins, was named by them Wingandocoa. "Their king is called Winginia," he added. Quick in her response, Elizabeth renamed the region *Virginia*—more agreeable to the cultured ear, a recognition that its new owner was the Virgin Queen, and an apt description for a land yet untouched and waiting to be possessed.

The Queen's successor, James I, in 1606 placed the coloniz-ing rights to that territory lying between the thirty-fourth and forty-first parallels in the ambitious hands of the London Company. The Crown and the Company especially desired the development of such river port towns as Alexandria. Two earlier settlements nearby, Dumfries and Colchester, began as thriving ports but declined as shallow harbors were heavily silted.

James had not chosen idealists to develop Virginia. The business of the London Company was to develop trade that would enrich England. In its use of the word, *trade* encom-passed fertile fields and rich harvests, wharves and warehouses serving a steady stream of merchant vessels, and settlers busy at producing exportable raw materials in exchange for prod-ucts manufactured in the homeland. All commerce would utilize English ships.

Indeed, after 1705 tobacco and naval stores were among the "enumerated commodities" that could be exported only to ports of the British empire. At this time, England, herself, urgently needed such commodities as tar, pitch, resin, flax, cordage, masts, yards, timber and other naval supplies. Also in demand from abroad were soap ash and glass which were being purchased from Russia and Poland, as these two coun-tries were rich in the vast timberland which England lacked; however, import duties were high. If England could procure from her Virginia colony such raw materials as these, shipped

Gilpin House and Chequire House continue to combine business on first floor with residences above.

in English vessels, in exchange for English goods, the economy would be well served.

In Virginia, the sentinel Capes of Henry and Charles guarded entrance to a tidewater land raveled and frayed along the shoreline by a maze of waterways, as yet unexplored by white men, that emptied into the inland sea called Chesapeake Bay. And at Cape Henry in April, 1607, the London Company made its first tenuous anchor-hold at point of entry into the great future of a New World. A few weeks later on May 13, at Jamestown, the first permanent English colony in North America was founded by the London Company with more than 100 colonists.

From this time, as the careful charting of rivers went on, the maps sent back to England were studied, and exploration plans formulated, the forward look was always northward from the guardian capes.

The largest and by far the most promising of the numerous rivers emptying into Chesapeake Bay was the Patowmeck or Potomac. On one of his visits back to England, Captain John Smith introduced the strange Indian name and reported that he had explored this great river about 125 miles inland to the Great Falls. The Indians from whom he learned the name seemed to associate the word with trading; and so Potomac came to be identified as "the trading river."

The Indians had been in Northern Virginia a very long time before the first white men came: at least ten thousand years by present-day scientific determination. The story of their long occupancy and of their progress from primitive hunters to artisans fashioning bows and arrows, making pottery and useful tools, and raising crops, is written in the charcoal of ancient fires, the graves of their dead, and the skeletons that are still discovered in the area.

The Potomac River was an estuary from two to eight miles wide as it was entered from the Bay. Back from its marshland shore as the river was followed inland there stretched un- limited acres of well-timbered land, how deep into the blue mountains only the Indians could say.

So promising were the reports spreading through the British Isles of opportunity offered in the new colony that there was scant spare space in any Virginia-bound ship. A typical report, widely distributed in England, describes Christmas in Virginia in 1613 thus: ". . . we were never more merry, nor fed on more plenty of good Oysters, Fish, Flesh, Wilde fowl and good bread, nor never had better fires in England."

This rich virgin land, in loosely-bounded and sketchily defined quantities, was readily available for grants to royal favorites by a monarch who had just begun to call his realm "Great" Britain. To James I, his colonial holdings seemed to be as inexhaustible as the air of his native Scotland or the waters encompassing his domain. These land grants were eagerly sought; for while Virginia was and would remain until the American Revolution a Crown colony, the Lords Proprietors were entitled to collect quitrents (taxes) from the settlers. In conjunction with the London Company the goal was development of this land for the enrichment of everyone concerned. Arrangements could be made to secure Virginia Land Patents in exchange for defraying the expenses of settlers who could not otherwise share in the opportunities the new land offered.

Among those who made such arrangements was a highly-connected, enterprising, Gloucester-born spinster named Margaret Brent. Since arriving at St. Mary's, Maryland, about 1638 and acquiring substantial holdings there, she had eyed with favor the Virginia shore where her brother Giles owned property; and arranged to bring fourteen settlers from England to the colony. In return for this service, in 1654, one Richard Bennett, Esq. did "give and grant . . . 700 acres of land . . . within ye freshes of Potomack River beginning at ye mouth of Hunting Creek . . ." to Margaret Brent. This historic land patent, which is still clearly legible, is in the Virginia State Archives, in Richmond. The document identifies a rectangular tract of land upon which a part of Old Alexandria now

OLDE TOWNE
CONFECTIONERY

ICE CREAM - CANDY

stands. The patent was reissued in 1662 by Sir William Berkeley, then Governor of Virginia, in these words: "The said land being formerly granted to said Brent by Patent dated the Sixth day of September One Thousand six hundred and fifty-four, and now renewed in his Majesties name . . ."

Seven years later, October 21, 1669, the same Sir William who, after some vicissitudes was still governor, granted to Robert Howsing (whose name is also spelled Howson, Howsen and Howseng) six thousand acres on the west bank of the Potomac. This man, described in one of the old records as a Welsh sea captain, obviously did not want the land for his own use. He sold it almost immediately to a Scotsman named John Alexander. There is some confusion in the genealogical records over the recurrence of given names in the Alexander line. Was this John Alexander who emigrated to Stafford County about 1640 or his son John? No matter to this story. There is ample evidence that John Alexander, as a surveyor, was familiar with the land described in the Howsing Patent of 1669. He knew how valuable this land was and he mightily wanted it. The price settled upon in the currency of the day was 6000 pounds of tobacco and the casks containing it. When the owner learned in clearing the title that the 700 acres of the earlier grant to Margaret Brent lay within his purchase, he valued the land enough to reimburse the heirs of the deceased Mistress Margaret with 10,500 pounds of tobacco plus casks. To a true Scotsman doubly-bought land was doubly dear. Long after his death in 1677, it was still known as "Alexander land," the rich inheritance of his numerous heirs. His name would in time be given to the town to be built upon a part of this land—Alexandria—where present day descendants continue to be as much a part of the old town as is the land itself.

As Virginia began to be settled, there was scant precedent for local government; so the House of Burgesses, which first met at Jamestown in 1619, set its own precedent, thus becoming the first representative legislature elected by popular vote.

New shops in old buildings on King Street.

It is often described as "the core of Anglo-American democracy."

These early and practical legislators who were in charge of colonial affairs were aware, as the records of their proceedings clearly indicate, that from the beginning many factors must enter into the development of a healthy economy—must combine to give meaning to the word permanent. With the groundwork of a sound legal structure achieved, they turned their attention to the economy. What could Virginia produce quickly and profitably that England would buy? The answer from both partners in the venture was the new crop called tobacco.

This weed was of West Indian origin, but the Indians had known about it long before America was discovered. It has been found in their pipes in archeological explorations that go back many centuries. But tobacco was unknown in England until Sir Walter Raleigh introduced it at the court of Queen Elizabeth. In Virginia, a young planter named John Rolfe, after experimenting with various native strains, harvested the first successful crop. He also discovered a method of curing it. In 1619 the first shipment of Virginia-grown tobacco (ten pounds!) was sent to England.

From that time on, the success of the tobacco economy depended upon the working together of three groups: the plantation owners of the increasingly extensive estates such as Mount Vernon and Gunston Hall on which exportable raw materials were raised; the import-export merchants, from the local representatives who were often younger members of merchant families, to the company executives in London and Glasgow; and the owners of shipping lines and captains of sailing vessels.

All three groups were aware of the urgency and necessity of developing river port towns with good harbor facilities. Pressure was brought to bear on the Virginia Assembly with the result that in 1680 authorization was given for the establishment of "rolling houses" and tobacco wharves at con-

Waterfront scene in the 1880s.

venient points on the rivers: the James, York, Rappahannock and Potomac. In 1691 a law was passed designating a public port in each county from which tobacco could be shipped. The terms *rolling house* and *rolling road* are descriptive of the way in which the 100-pound hogsheads of cured tobacco were brought from field to wharf. They were literally rolled along, often on the old Indian trails, thus hard-packing the first colonial roads.

Warehouses in which the tobacco could be stored against spoilage, and wharves where it could be inspected and loaded for the first stage of the long journey across the ocean to market, sprouted fast along the waterways. Around many of them clustered small communities.

On the Potomac the site that was to become Alexandria

Waterfront scene, houses on South Lee Street in distance.
From the collection of O. Ashby Reardon, used by permission of Mrs. Reardon.

offered by far the best port potential. Here there was harbor space to accommodate the ocean-going cargo vessels of the times: full-rigged ships frequently under 150 tons. A typical Virginia-built topsail schooner for foreign trade, prior to the Revolutionary War, was perhaps no more than 50 feet long on deck, 13 or 14 feet wide, and would have listed at about 50 tons. In a single decade (1800–1810) in Alexandria alone a dozen such vessels were built and outfitted. Their total capacity was about 1,500 tons.

At the terminus of Oronoco Trail, in the present vicinity of Oronoco and North Fairfax streets, there had been warehouse sheds and some form of wharf for a long time. In 1730 the General Assembly directed that a warehouse be established south of Hunting Creek, that is, south of the present Woodrow Wilson Bridge. When this location proved to be unsuitable, a rolling house was built on the upper side of Great Hunting Creek. This was a public warehouse for inspection, storage and shipment of tobacco, and was soon connected with the Maryland shore by a public ferry. Most of the settlers in the small community that grew around these facilities were Scottish. English merchants were engaged in business in the colony, too, but in general they were reluctant to come with their families from a comfortable life at home to the hazards of a new land. In contrast, many Scots, Lowlanders for the large part, found the climate and commercial prospects of Virginia an agreeable exchange for their stony fields and hard existence. The Act of Union between England and Scotland, passed in 1707, accelerated the flow of Scottish immigration. Old loyalties and old customs came with all the settlers. Those in the Hunting Creek community called the settlement Belhaven. Thus they honored the Earl of Belhaven, forceful opponent and dramatic orator in the fight against union between Scotland and England. Although his efforts failed, his admirers in Virginia recognized him as a true son of liberty and a fallen martyr in a lost cause.

Visitors from other sections of the country may be surprised to learn that very few Virginia communities with colonial origins began as spontaneous settlements of two or three dwellings around a church, a fort or at a crossroads. Towns like Alexandria were planned and were authorized by law, on land appropriated for the purpose, according to a town plan laid out on paper and, in the case of Alexandria, given a name—all before a single tree had been felled or the underbrush cleared from a potential building site.

FOUNDING OF ALEXANDRIA JULY 13, 1749

Petitions for such a town at the mouth of Hunting Creek on the Potomac went down to the General Assembly at Williamsburg from planters and merchants alike. The arguments they presented made good sense. As a result the Assembly agreed, in 1748, that the town for which it was so assiduously petitioned "would be commodious for trade and navigation, and tend greatly to the ease and advantage of the frontier inhabitants . . ."

By official act, a 60-acre tract of Alexander land, then belonging to Philip Alexander, John Alexander (namesake of the original owner), and Hugh West, a member of the family by marriage, was set aside for the town. The tract was to begin "at the mouth of the first branch above the warehouse (Orinoka Creek) and extend down the meanders of the Potomac . . . and back into the woods" to the quantity specified. No matter that the small settlement had for several years been called Belhaven. The name would be quickly forgot as the town of Alexandria emerged. The land was to be surveyed, divided into blocks in a gridiron pattern by streets, cut into half-acre lots, and auctioned for prompt development—all within a specified time limit: four months. Eleven of the chief petitioners were duly appointed to serve as directors and trustees "for designing, building, carrying on and maintaining the said town." It was to be located on the south bank of Potomac River, well below the Great Falls, and about five miles south of the marshland and meadows on the opposite side where, in time, the city of Washington would be built. When the lots were sold, the trustees were to reimburse the owners whose sixty acres had been appropriated.

The Authorization Act stated in effect: "You wanted a town here. You may have it—to build and to run." And that is precisely what the first eleven trustees and their successors did until 1779. At that time, Alexandria was incorporated and a mayor and city council were elected. The last of the trustees to be appointed was a man who always claimed Alexandria as his home town: George Washington.

As the night mist lifted off the river on that July morning in 1749 and the rising sun came on a path of gold to the small clearing where a new town was to begin that day, the 142 years of history that had foreordained the founding of Alexandria became prologue.

Today in Market Square at the center and heart of Old Alexandria you and I can, if we like, stand about and try to reconstruct the scene on that first auction day.

Announcements of the auction have been made in all the colonial gazettes. Handbills have been distributed and "the word" has gone out far and wide throughout tidewater Virginia. Even before the day itself, every road and trail leading from the back country toward the small clearing near the river where the bidding will take place could be traced between fields of deep-greening tobacco by the dust of horsemen galloping along, of the carriages of the gentry rocking comfortably, and the wagonloads of more humble colonists. And on the riverfront, sloops and shallops and brigantines, every variety of water craft, vie for docking space at the wharf or tie up in adjacent coves.

Nobody with the conscientious zeal of a Tobias Lear (Washington's faithful companion and secretary) sits on a freshly cut stump in the center of Alexandria-to-be with notebook and pencil. But within three years when the first fair days are held in the same place, many of the same persons attending the auction will leave descriptions of comparable gatherings.

The horses have been unhitched from the carriages, wagons and carts and led to a cool place away from the crowd. Buckets of fresh spring water with wooden or tin dippers are put in place. There are hampers of food and perhaps the aroma of freshly-caught fish as they broil over a few coals.

As the crowd gathers, John West is the man to watch. He will give the signal for the start of the bidding and serve as auctioneer. The spring has been a busy time for this county surveyor. Accompanied often by his young apprentice, 17-year-old George Washington, he has scrambled through the underbrush, waded in the marshlands, fought off insects and watched for snakes as he covered every square foot of the 60-acre tract. Washington is easy to locate in the crowd. Russet of hair, with broad shoulders and large, capable hands,

At a Meeting of the Majority of the Trustees of Alexandria
Town July the 13th 1749

Present. Richard Osborn.   John Pagan

William Ramsay.   Gerard Alexander

John Carlyle.   &   Hugh West. Gent.

John West Sen.r appointed Clerk of this Town in order to keep an
count of the proceedings.

And appointed Cryer at the sales of the Lotts.

It is agreed that the Lotts be sold at Publick Vendue within five Minutes
from the time that they are set to sale.

Then Proceeded to sell the Lotts as Followeth. Viz.

No.		Sold		Pistoles
36	Sold	John Dalton		19
31		Gerard Alexander		19 1/2
26		Allan Macrae		22
41		John Carlyle		30
46		William Ramsay		30
51		Laurence Washington		31
20 & 21		Roger Lindon		45 1/2
1		William Fitzhugh		26 1/2
2		John Pagan		10 1/2
56 & 57	Hon.ble	William Fairfax		35
62 & 63	Coll.o	George Fairfax		39
69 & 70	Coll.o	Nathaniel Harrison		46
77 & 78		Nathaniel Chapman		56 1/2
32		Gerard Alexander		20
27		John Alexander		8
37		John Dalton		16
42		John Carlyle		16
52		Laurence Washington		16
47		William Ramsay		16

(1)

he is already a head taller than many of the men. In a sense, this day is a beginning for him, too, for in short time he will qualify as a surveyor himself, begin to earn his own money, and become increasingly his own man. What lies ahead for George Washington on this auction day is as time-shrouded as the distant Maryland shore where a nation's capital will bear his name.

The gridiron plan is marked out on the 60-acre tract by raw poplar stakes. There are to be ten streets, each 66 feet wide. Six of the seven running westward from the river are given the conventional names of the first streets in many colonial towns: King and Queen, Prince and Princess, Duke and Duchess. The seventh is Cameron which honors Thomas, sixth Lord Fairfax who is also Baron of Cameron, and the largest landowner in the colony. The three cross-streets running north and south are Water Street, nearest the river, then Fairfax Street and Royal Street. Within the blocks of the grid they form are the lots that are to be put up for sale, four to each block. Eight of the original streets will keep their names. In time, Water Street will become Lee Street. As for Duchess, it is the old Oronoco Trail, worn through the woods by so many Indian moccasins in long-gone years and more recently pounded hard by tobacco casks rolled to water. The old name sticks, and that is why Alexandria has no Duchess Street except on early maps.

One such map is being prepared by George Washington to send to his older half-brother, Lawrence, who is away on business in England. The other half-brother, Augustine, is here from Mount Vernon, commissioned to buy lots for Lawrence and eager to select other choice ones for himself.

The eleven new trustees are all here today, in person or by proxy or agent, for all have their eyes on the lots they wish to purchase except for Thomas, sixth Lord Fairfax. These are important men, handsomely attired, well supplied with Spanish pistoles, the popular coin of the day. They have agreed, as the first page of the minute book spells out clearly, that "the lots

Minutes of meeting of trustees, July 13, 1749, are still legible.

be sold at public vendue within five minutes from the time they are set to sale," and that John West should serve as Cryer.

With his signal, the bidding begins. John Dalton, a Scottish merchant and one of the trustees, successfully bids on the first lot, No. 36. Gerard Alexander, descendant of the first John Alexander, now long gone, bids for No. 31, and later counts himself fortunate to get No. 32 also. No man is allowed to have more than two lots on this first day. When the day's activities are over, Dalton, Alexander, John Carlyle, William Ramsay, Lawrence Washington, William Fairfax, and Col. George William Fairfax have their quota.

On the following morning the scene is re-enacted as the auction continues. By nightfall, George Mason, from Gunston Hall, and Col. William Fitzhugh, from Chatham, are among the leaders of Northern Virginia who own two lots each. As the crowd disperses on the second day of bidding, forty-one of the now well-trampled lots have owners, and two have been reserved for Market Square and the town hall.

Augustine Washington quickly pens a letter to his brother Lawrence giving an account of the day's business when he learns that a packet is ready to sail for England. This letter, located among the Washington papers in the Library of Congress some years ago by an Alexandria historian, whose own old house stands on one of the first lots sold, is partly torn, but brings back vividly the scene:

"I purchased you two lots near the water upon the Main street as everyone along the rode will be through that street." The riverside lots, he writes, were set up first and were purchased "at a very extravagant price."

Almost immediately after the auction the town began to take shape. The Founding Act set forth clearly specific regulations: within two years of purchase the owner of every lot was to "erect, build and finish . . . one house of brick, stone or wood well framed of the dimensions of twenty feet square . . ." and if this was not done, the lot would be reinvested in the

At a Meeting of the Majority of The Trustees of the Town of Alexandria the 13th Day of July 1759.

Present. G: W.m Fairfax.   x George. Mason.
         George Johnston.   Robert. Adam.
         John. Hunter.   John Muir.
                                       Ger.d Alexander.

On the representation of John Carlyle & John Dalton that a g.n & convenient Landing at Cameron Street in the Town of Alexandria may be made of General Utility to the Town and that they will undertake to accomplish the same provided they and their Heirs in Consequence of the expence they will be at may have leave to apply to their use one half of the said Landing the same being Considered by the Trustees leave is granted to the said John Carlyle & John Dalton to execute the same & to appropriate one half thereof to their use as a landing

G.e W.m Fairfax
G. Mason
G. Johnston
John Hunter
Robert Adam
John Muir
Ger.d Alexander

Agreed to

Old minutes show how the town began to grow.

trustees to be sold to others who would comply with the requirements.

Alexandria's first building boom was beginning. Warehouses, sail lofts, rope walks and shipyards were under way on the bank of the Potomac. Shops proliferated, often with the family quarters of the owner occupying the upper floors. Taverns and inns offered accommodations and entertainment for visiting seamen. And soon, the half-acre lots began to be divided into smaller lots on which were erected town houses adjacent to each other with gardens stretching to the rear.

As early as 1752 the town trustees began exercising their authority with these additional regulations which in themselves reflect the rapid growth of the town:

". . . *all dwelling houses from this day not begun or to be built hereafter shall be built on the front and be in line with the street as chief of the houses now are, and that no gable or end of such house be on or next to the Street, except an angle or where two streets cross, otherwise to be pulled down.*"

These regulations together with all the minutes of the regular monthly meetings of the trustees through the years are among the archives treasured in the present Alexandria City Hall.

The town was developing so rapidly that in 1762 the trustees requested permission from the General Assembly to enlarge its area. The request was granted and on May 9, 1763, forty-six additional lots were offered for public auction. On the thirtieth anniversary of its founding, in 1779, Alexandria was incorporated as a town. By that time, its territory had been extended westward to include Washington Street, which was to be 100 feet wide. Thereafter, the names of the streets in themselves tell much about the history of the times: Wolfe, for the British general who won a victory over the French at Quebec; Wilkes after a member of the British Parliament who suffered for his stout defense of the colonies; Pitt after the British Prime Minister who was a lover of liberty; St. Asaph after the Bishop of St. Asaph who wrote in defense of liberty for the colonists and in whose home Benjamin Franklin began writing his autobiography. And then came Washington, Jefferson, Franklin, two streets, Patrick and Henry, and Lee.

The streets of Old Alexandria are modern today; but as you walk along them, you will be constantly in company with the illustrious names and events from America's history.

2 Walking Tours through Old Town

This section contains directions for four walking tours in Old Alexandria:

Landmarks in Use: Public buildings

Houses Associated with Distinguished Personages and Events: Fourteen houses

Houses with a Past and a Presence: Flounder houses—Captains Row—Gentry Row—Alley houses—Houses with special architectural interest

Old Churches and Cemeteries: Christ Episcopal Church—Old Presbyterian Meeting House—St. Mary's Roman Catholic Church—Alexandria National Cemetery

Limited free parking for visitors is provided at George Washington Bicentennial Headquarters (Lyceum), 201 South Washington Street, open 7 days a week 9 a.m. to 5 p.m.

Parking permits for out-of-city visitors to use metered spaces without charge are available upon request at Ramsay House, Alexandria Tourist Center, corner King and North Fairfax Streets, open daily 10 a.m. to 4:30 p.m. (closed Sunday).

Maps, literature and general assistance to visitors are available at both centers.

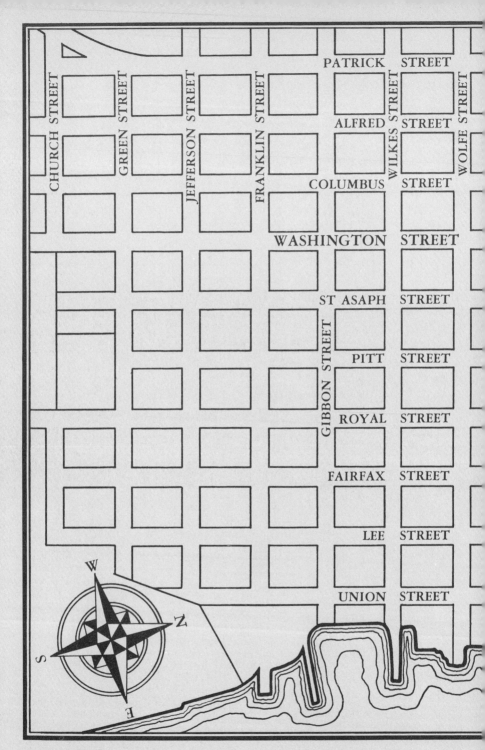

Map of Old Town

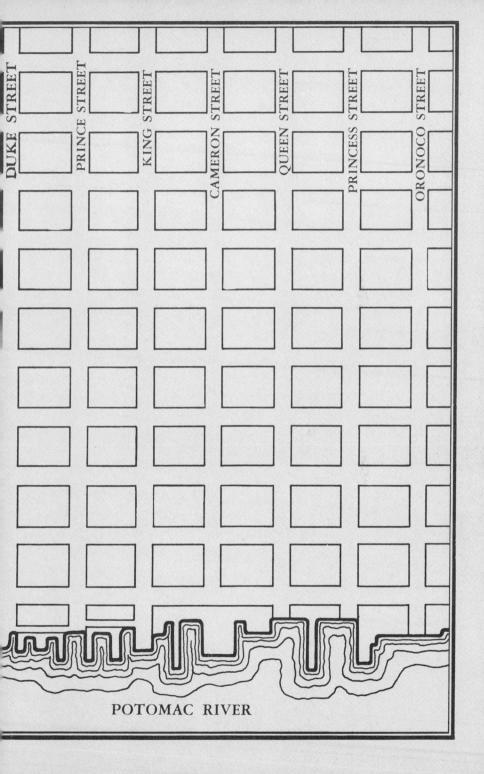

DUKE STREET

PRINCE STREET

KING STREET

CAMERON STREET

QUEEN STREET

PRINCESS STREET

ORONOCO STREET

POTOMAC RIVER

TOUR ONE
1 to 2 hours

Landmarks in Use

THE historic landmarks visited on this tour are public buildings that have been in service as such for approximately one hundred and fifty years. All continue to serve and are open to the public without charge except as, from time to time, renovation requires temporary closing. The Tour begins at the Alexandria Lyceum, now serving as the George Washington Northern Virginia Bicentennial Center, 201 South Washington Street, open seven days a week from 9 a.m. to 5 p.m. The route is arranged geographically and concludes at the Athenaeum, 201 Prince Street. At the end of the description of each building, directions are given for reaching the next one.

43

Gadsby's Tavern, handsomely furnished and appointed.

THE LYCEUM (Bicentennial Center)
201 South Washington Street

Open seven days a week 9 a.m. to 5 p.m. · Museum, displays, gift shop · No admission charge.

The Lyceum, completed in 1839 and long the center of cultural life in the community, is one of the few Greek Revival buildings erected in Alexandria, where the prevailing architecture of early structures is Georgian, Federal and later, Victorian. It is indeed one of few built anywhere in Virginia.

The Lyceum was designed and constructed to serve the purpose its classical style and name indicate: a hall, often replete with marble busts of great philosophers and debaters, as was this one, in which lectures, concerts and the like are presented. Prior to its construction, two cultural groups were active in the community, each using such facilities as were available to meet their needs. One was the Alexandria Lyceum Company, which was organized in 1834 under the inspiration and leadership of the Quaker schoolmaster, Benjamin Hallowell. The other was the Alexandria Library Company, a subscription organization, meeting first at Old Presbyterian Meeting House, with Dr. James Muir, the pastor, as first president, and existing without interruption since 1794. Cooperatively the two groups purchased the land on which the Lyceum stands, and for many years occupied the building jointly. The Alexandria Library used the first floor which consisted of a reading room and various historical and archeological displays. The second floor consisted of a large public room where the Lyceum Society held its meetings. It was also used for concerts, dances and other social affairs, in much the same way the room is used today.

The Lyceum was requisitioned, as were many buildings in Alexandria, for use as a hospital during the Civil War when the city was occupied by Union forces. After the war, it was sold and renovated to serve as a private residence; and it is still as the McGuire House that many older residents refer to the building. In 1940 the Lyceum was sold again, this time to be used as an office building. In the handsome old rooms doctors and lawyers and such organizations as the Alexandria Chamber of Commerce found comfortable quarters; however, the old building was feeling the burden of its years. As tenants moved to more modern locations, the handsome Doric columns and interior woodwork were allowed to deteriorate. The building faced danger of demolition when, in 1969, the City of Alexandria, acting with historic initiative and independence, exercised the unprecedented right, for a local Virginia community, of *eminent domain* to preserve it. This is the constitutional right by which a government, federal, state, county or municipal, can intervene to condemn privately owned property, indemnify the owners, and use the property to serve the best interests of the people. Funds to purchase and restore the Lyceum for its present use were provided by the City of Alexandria, the Department of Housing and Urban Development, the Department of the Interior, the State of Virginia, the Alexandria Association for Restoration and Preservation and many public spirited individuals.

The building is a center where you may learn much about colonial American history and Old Alexandria through a series of well planned three-dimensional exhibits and tape recordings. It is in a sense a journey backward through time, beginning with an introduction to "a special breed of men who, by the circumstances of their time and place" belonged first to colonial Northern Virginia, then to the new nation they struggled to bring forth, and now, they belong to all Americans for all time.

The first of these men to meet is an English-born nobleman, Thomas sixth Lord Fairfax and Baron of Cameron. He was still a student at Oxford University when he inherited through his mother the Virginia territory known as the Northern Neck, lying between the Potomac and Rappahannock rivers. Thus, he became Lord Proprietor of a land grant which he

increased to more than *five million acres* of virtually unsettled and in some part very wild frontier territory. After visiting Virginia from 1735 to 1737, Lord Fairfax determined to return, to make his home here permanently, and to devote his life to the development of his holdings.

He went first to Belvoir Manor, the estate of a cousin, Colonel William Fairfax. This was near Mount Vernon where young George Washington was making his home with the Lawrence Washington family. The tall, almost gaunt aristocrat, with his beaked nose and passion for good horseflesh, particularly hunters, took a liking to the tall lad who had lost his father at any early age. The two began with a mutual interest in surveying. Then, as they rode to hounds or explored the countryside, Lord Fairfax imparted to George Washington, whose formal education was limited, much information and experience that would influence his later life.

Lord Fairfax soon moved westward in his domain, establishing himself at a lodge which he called Greenway Court, near Winchester, Va. Washington's first visit to the site of Greenway Court was in the early spring of 1748 when he had just turned sixteen. In his diary, that lifetime record he was to keep faithfully until the night before his death, he recorded: "Saturday, March 12th—This morning Mr. James Genn ye surveyor came to us (Washington and Lord Fairfax) we travel'd over ye Blue Ridge to Capt. Ashby's on Shannondoah River. Nothing remarkable happen'd. Sunday, March 13—Rode to his Lordship's Quarters about 4 miles higher up ye River . . ." Here at Greenway Court into his eighty-ninth year lived the nobleman Washington customarily referred to as "the dear old Lord." He was popular with the families that had settled on his land, in the saddle often from dawn to dusk in all kinds of weather, busy with the administration of his extensive affairs. He saw the colonialism which he represented decline, and watched with profound regret the growth of a new spirit of independence from England. Lord Fairfax was the only English nobleman unfailingly loyal to his king and country who was allowed to spend all the turbulent years of the American Revolution, unmolested, living quietly in retirement on his long-held property. On October 19, 1781, at Yorktown, his friend George Washington, General of the Continental Army, defeated the English army under Lord Cornwallis. A few weeks later, at Greenway Court, the old Lord Proprietor breathed his last. His beloved property fell heir by confiscation to the state he had done so much to develop—enough land to be divided in time into twenty-one counties.

The age of the colonial planter comes to life in the exhibit through a combination of portraits, lighted color photographs of great houses as they are today, actual furniture of the period and personal possessions. These include a pair of silver shoe buckles, fine china from the tea table, books left open from the last reading and others in which quill-penned records have been preserved. You are invited, in a sense, to come for a visit to see for yourself what life was like on a colonial Virginia estate.

First, there is Kenmore, the home of George Washington's sister, Betty, and her husband, Fielding Lewis, in Fredericksburg. You can look through an open door into the colorful garden of this mansion. At Gunston Hall, the home of George Mason, near Mount Vernon, you go into the dining room where the table is set for guests. Through an imposing doorway, there is a good view of the work of the great master of interior architecture, William Buckland, who began his career in America as an indentured servant on this estate. Then, while visiting Mount Vernon, you find a comfortable old rocker drawn up close to the library window which looks out toward the working part of a colonial plantation.

Life for the planter was more than silks and satins, lace flounces at the wrist, knee breeches and silver-buckled shoes. His day often began early at a handsome secretary-desk such as the one you see here. A sheaf of papers on the open desk, a tricorn hat and cane on the chair, bespeak the urgency of business outside: at the mill where flour and meal are ground, in the workshop where barrels and wagons and farming implements are being made, in the stables where horse-power means well-kept animals. In this part of the exhibit, many of the tools that were actually worn smooth by use are suspended from the rafters.

There is real Virginia tobacco lying on top a handmade barrel. The dark green leaves of fresh tobacco, after being cut from the stalk, are gathered into "hands," each skillfully wrapped at the stem end with a tobacco leaf, and then cured in barns and sheds. This barrel is much smaller than the great hogsheads of the same shape in which 100 pounds of tobacco could be packed and then rolled from field to shipping points along the creeks and rivers. The weathered old ropes and floats in this exhibit are reminders that Old Alexandria was the chief shipping point for Virginia tobacco and other raw products.

In the next exhibit, against a muraled wall, you may feel that you are really on an eighteenth-century street in Old Town. The horses drawing vehicles and the people walking along the old streets seem to be alive. There are replicas of signs that identify such establishments as the Rising Sun Tavern and the Stabler Apothecary Shop. They swing above displays of pewter mugs and plates, a worn mortar and pestle, stained medicine bottles, a curious double-wick lamp, a mold in which the fine silver spoons made in Alexandria were cast.

The exhibits you have seen are an introduction to Old Alexandria. You can discover the past in the present wherever you go in the modern city outside.

To visit the next Landmark in Use walk west (left) from the Lyceum on Prince Street to South Alfred Street. Turn right to:

FRIENDSHIP FIRE ENGINE COMPANY
107 South Alfred Street

Open Tuesday through Saturday 10 a.m. to 4 p.m. · No admission charge.

Small boys and small-boys-at-heart who love red fire engines will be particularly attracted to the present home of generations of historic fire-fighting equipment used in Old Alexandria. Here in the center of modern Alexandria, blocks westward from the early buildings it once protected, is housed the town's first fire engine. A guide in colonial costume is on hand every day to tell about it.

A volunteer fire company was organized August 5, 1774, with George Washington as a member. The following year, when General Washington went to Philadelphia to take command of the Continental Army, he bought a fire engine at his own expense (about $400) as a gift for the townspeople here. It was transported from Philadelphia to Alexandria by ox cart, and housed first at Rainbow Tavern, located at the end of Sharpshin Alley, which ran from Royal Street south to Fairfax Street.

On display with it is a hand pump engine made in 1849 and a hose reel, built in Alexandria the same year, and used in connection with the hand pumper. There are also leather fire buckets, helmets, and other interesting equipment used through the years.

During the Bicentennial Celebration, everyone throughout the country who visits the Freedom Train as it makes its way from city to city will have an opportunity to see one of the old fire engines from Alexandria.

The date 1774 conspicuously displayed on the front of the building refers to the organization of the first company. It is headquarters for the Friendship Veterans Fire Engine Company which uses the upper floor for various ceremonial occasions.

50

Home of the fire engine Washington
purchased for the town.

The first fire engine and its successors were kept in a number of convenient and available locations through the years; and their lot was not always so pleasant and comfortable as it is today. Indeed, when the little Washington engine was old and outdated after years of faithful service, it was sold to a succession of junk dealers. In 1849, the engine was "discovered" by the Veteran Firemen's Association of Baltimore, Maryland, bought as a prized antique, and added to its museum. There it remained for a century—a part of Alexandria's historic past, in exile. Then, in 1954, on February 22, after much persuasive negotiations, the fire engine came home where it belongs. The present building, dating, itself, to 1855, was dedicated as a National Shrine in honor of Washington.

The loving care given to the old engines which always gleam with polished brass and fresh red paint is made possible by business leaders in the community who perpetuate the first volunteer fire company, although they have long ago relinquished fire-fighting responsibilities to the City Fire Department.

From the Fire House, walk north on S. Alfred Street to King Street. Turn east (right) and walk 5 blocks to Royal Street. Turn left on Royal Street to end of block to:

GADSBY'S TAVERN
132 North Royal Street (Corner Cameron Street)

Closed for restoration 1975 and early 1976 · Temporary office of the Curator, 200 North Royal Street. Formal opening of the restored Gadsby's Tavern, including dining room and house museum, is scheduled as a part of the 1976 Washington's Birthday Celebration.

Everything happens at Gadsby's!

Such has been the life-story of this historic Tavern from the day the first and smaller of the two sections was completed and opened when Alexandria was a small, new town.

Gadsby's Tavern today.
Courtesy the curator, Gadsby's Tavern.

The sign "closed temporarily for restoration" is but the beginning of a new chapter in the story, and an invitation to return soon when the restoration work has been completed. At that time, a measure of the hospitality and service for which this old hostelry had a world famous reputation in its heyday will be resumed.

The Tavern began as Mason's Ordinary, a term used at the time to describe an inn where the charge for food, lodging and stableage was fixed each year by the court. Through a succession of owners and tavernkeepers during the latter part of the eighteenth century it was known by a variety of names: Fountain Tavern, the Bunch of Grapes (when an identifying sign was moved to this building from a tavern across the street which was operated by the same innkeeper), as the City

53

An inventory of the furnishings of the Tavern in 1777 indicates
the elegance of its appointments.

Courtesy the Library of Congress and curator, Gadsby's Tavern.

Tavern and City Hotel. But from 1795 when the building
was leased by John Gadsby, it has been, and hereafter always
will be *Gadsby's*. The handsome John Gadsby never owned
the building; however, his name was synonymous with the
elegant appointments and lavish hospitality that gave the
Tavern its reputation. Authors Deering Davis and Stephen
Palmer Dorsey, in their study of Alexandria Houses done in
1946, declare Gadsby's Tavern to be the "finest tavern in the
colonies built before 1800." They quote an English Arch-
bishop traveling in Virginia who said such "ordinaries were
kept by gentlemen and that only such were entertained."

The older of the two buildings comprising the Tavern as
it stands today belongs to the very early history of Alexandria.
The doorway to this building (the second from the corner
of North Royal and Cameron Streets) is particularly notable.

It has Doric pilasters supporting a superb pediment with dentiled cornice. It has been termed "the finest one of wood in Virginia."

The vicissitudes of this handsome doorway alone are worth recording. A half-century ago the old building fell upon hard times. The doorway was sold to the Metropolitan Museum of Art to be used in its then new American Wing. There it remained until plans began to take shape for the observance in 1949 of the Bicentennial of the Founding of Alexandria. Then, a public-spirited couple who had recently restored one of the nearby eighteenth century "great houses," negotiated for its return, and presented the doorway as a birthday gift, both to Gadsby's Tavern and to the residents of Alexandria. The doorway was carefully replaced in its proper position where it will remain to welcome a new generation of guests.

The large three-story building on the corner was added by one of the early owners, John Wise. The difference in the appearance of the bricks shows clearly where the two buildings were joined. The formal opening was held in February 1793 of the "new and elegant Three-Story Brick House, fronting the West end of the Market House, which was built for a Tavern, and has twenty commodious, well furnished rooms in it where he (John Wise) has laid in a large stock of good old Liquors, and hopes he will be able to give satisfaction to all who may please to favor him with their custom."

On the second floor of the new building was an exceedingly handsome ballroom, complete with musicians' balcony, where most of the important large social events of Alexandria took place. Although the front doorway to the smaller building came back to Alexandria, the interior of the ballroom, which was also purchased by the Metropolitan Museum, remains there, with such memories and nostalgia as may be the lot of old wood and old associations. The ballroom was authentically reproduced a half century ago and, by the time the building was closed for restoration, had, itself, acquired such an air of belonging that few natives would have it otherwise.

John Gadsby,
always the
gracious host.
Courtesy the curator,
Gadsby's Tavern.

A very important part of the building that was rarely seen by its guests was a brick-walled underground ice-house which was filled every winter when the ice from the river was considered to be "right" with great blocks which were lowered from Cameron Street through a chute. Packed in straw, the ice could be removed in required quantities by access from the basement down a narrow flight of steps. When the present restoration program is complete, visitors will be able to look into the ice-house from the sidewalk through a viewing chamber.

During the latter part of the eighteenth and early part of the nineteenth century, Gadsby's Tavern was by no means the only one in Alexandria. There were at least a dozen popular inns and taverns in addition to coffee houses and lodging places on the waterfront. Of these, however, Gadsby's is the only one to retain its identity and to substantiate its story.

The tavern was important, first of all, to travelers of the day. Alexandria was at the crossroads of Colonial America— the terminus and point of departure of the great highways of the country. From the stone paved courtyard here went all the northbound coaches to Georgetown, Philadelphia, New York and Boston; the southbound ones to Williamsburg, Richmond, Charleston and New Orleans. Highways they were, indeed: King's Highway, Potomac Path, Glebe Road, Leesburg Pike, Braddock Road, Little River Turnpike. The King's Highway began on Chesapeake Bay between the York and James rivers. It extended northward along "the path of the aborigines up the backbone of the peninsula" through Williamsburg, thence by Bowling Green, Fredericksburg, Stafford Court House, Dumfries and Colchester . . . then "wound by Washington's mill, close by Mount Vernon, through the Ford at Cameron Run and down into Alexandria." The "Great Highway" from Colchester on Occoquam Creek to Alexandria is described in an old journal as "surely the most treacherous" stretch of road in all Virginia, going through a swamp and fording streams or runs that in rainy weather could suddenly turn into raging torrents.

Trust Charles Dickens in his *American Notes* for the best description of a journey across the Potomac down to Fredericksburg: "Soon after nine o'clock we came to Potomac Creek, where we are to land, and then comes the oddest part of the journey. Seven stage-coaches are preparing to carry us on . . . There are four horses to each coach . . . the coaches are something like the French coaches, but not nearly so good. In lieu of springs, they are hung on bands of the strongest leather . . . They are covered with mud from roof to wheel tyre, and have never been cleaned since they were built.

"The first half-mile of the road is over bridges made of loose planks laid across two parallel poles, which tilt up as the wheels roll over them and *in* the river. The river has a clayey bottom and is full of holes, so that half a horse is constantly disappearing, and can't be found again for some time."

Two young foreign aristocrats who, according to old stories, traveled such a route on horseback well into dusk of a summer evening in 1777, were particularly grateful for the sight of the town of Alexandria where, at the tavern, they had arranged to take fresh mounts. This was the first visit to Alexandria of the Marquis de Lafayette, 23 years old then, and according to a statement later made by General Nathanael Greene, a young man "determined to be in the way of danger." His companion that night was a Bavarian, whether Baron DeKalb or soldier of fortune. Both these young Europeans were on their way to Philadelphia to volunteer their services to the Continental Army. Their command of English was so limited that they could not explain adequately to the tavernkeeper that they needed lodging, food and fresh mounts. At this point, a handsome 30-year-old naval officer named John Paul Jones came to the rescue. Presently, dinner was arranged, the wine was excellent and friendships were begun.

An inventory of the contents of the Tavern made at that time gives some idea of the furniture and furnishings it contained. Here are a few of the items: walnut tables, including an oval one with carved feet and a tea table, a set of 16 leather-bottomed chairs, five china punch bowls, two of them "delph" and two Queens China, two punch ladles, blue and white china plates, cups and saucers and a silver cream pot, 7 glass decanters, 3 brass chafing dishes, a tea kettle stand, lime squeezers and a cork screw, 30 gallons of rum, 9 gallons of brandy, a corner cupboard, 4 sets of iron firedogs, silver teaspoons and tablespoons, bedspreads and a silk quilt, sheets and blankets, pillows and bolsters, chamber pots and an old riding chair, 2 gallons of "Ginn" and 2 bushels of salt.

The hospitality, comforts and appointments of the Tavern were immeasurably improved after its management passed to

John Gadsby, an Englishman. Though he described himself as of "meager" background, there was no end to his accomplishments and abilities as an inn keeper. His first venture in Alexandria was a waterfront tavern and coffee house where he catered to customers from the ships tied up at the wharves. In 1796 he signed a six-year lease with John Wise for the new corner building on Royal and Cameron Streets. When he renewed the lease in 1802, it included the adjoining older coffee house, thus bringing together under one management the two hostelries whose history thereafter was to be one story.

The fame of Gadsby's Tavern spread far and wide. The guest register, had it survived, would have contained the autographs of five presidents of the United States: George Washington, John Adams, Thomas Jefferson, James Madison and John Quincy Adams, also George Mason, John Marshall, Alexander Hamilton, Benjamin Franklin, Aaron Burr, Benjamin Latrobe, architect of the National Capitol; Francis Scott Key, shortly before he composed the *Star Spangled Banner;* Henry Clay, John C. Calhoun and, if the whole truth be told, on one occasion, with considerable lifting of local eyebrows, Eng and Chang Bunker. These were the original Siamese twins, joined at the hip, who were brought to this country as circus attractions and who, eventually, married sisters and settled on adjoining farms just across the Virginia border in North Carolina. By this time, as you may suspect, John Gadsby had long since left Alexandria for Washington where his entertaining and entertainment capacities continued to be developed.

Not all the guests who came to Gadsby's Tavern introduced themselves accurately to the host. There was, for instance, the well-bred young couple arriving one autumn day by ship from the West Indies. They took a carriage to the tavern where the young woman, obviously sick, was put to bed. A doctor was called; and as her condition worsened, Mrs. John Duffey, wife of a silversmith, who lived nearby on South

Fairfax Street, and another neighbor took turns at nursing. The details of the story which have accumulated through a century and a half of telling are varied. But the fact remains that she died, and was buried in the graveyard of St. Paul's Episcopal Church, where she still lies. Her companion ordered a handsome bench-type marble monument, for which allegedly he never paid, on which this inscription is carved:

> To the Memory of a
> FEMALE STRANGER
> whose mortal suffering terminated
> on the 14th day of October 1816
> Aged 23 years and 8 months
> This stone is placed by her disconsolate
> husband in whose arms she sighed out her
> latest breath and who under God
> did his utmost even to soothe the cold
> dead ear of death
> How loved, how valued once avails thee not,
> To whom related, or by whom begot.
> A heap of dust alone remains of thee
> 'Tis all thou art and all the proud shall be.
> To Him gave all the Prophets witness that
> through His name whosoever believeth in
> Him shall receive remission of sins.

Four of the lines might be considered more nearly biographical were they not a part of the classical education of every student of the works of Alexander Pope.

As for the two women who tended the stranger night and day throughout her illness, could they identify her? To the end of their days, they affirmed that indeed they could. But women are good at keeping secrets. Their silence proved the point.

The small, white-walled second floor front bedchamber in which this romantic tragedy was enacted has ever since been known as "The Female Stranger's Room." It has been suitably furnished and is maintained by the John Alexander Chapter, Daughters of the American Revolution.

Bedroom of Female Stranger.
Courtesy John Alexander Chapter, NSDAR.

Many of the legends that are a part of the tradition of Gadsby's Tavern are at best sketchily authenticated; but old buildings are entitled to their legends and their ghosts; and to the eternal mystery both create.

To the residents of Alexandria and their friends from the neighboring plantations, Gadsby's Tavern was the center of social and civic life. Here were held balls and banquets and dancing parties, concerts and celebrations of all sorts of important events, meetings of the St. Andrew's Society, the Jockey Club, lottery drawings, theatrical performances and cockfights in the courtyard.

There is some doubt about whether a youthful George Washington actually left his bootprints on the topmost stone step of the smaller of the tavern buildings on March 19, 1754, when he accepted his commission as a lieutenant colonel in the Virginia Militia; but none at all about the fact that in October, 1755, he paid for lodgings there.

Forty-three years later, in 1798, when the aging Washington was on his way home to Mount Vernon from Philadelphia, the Independent Blues, that great military organization of such distinguished service which has recently been reactivated, with proper uniforms and equipment for ceremonial occasions, met their beloved General-President outside the town. They escorted him to the Tavern where the dinner he ordered on that day is a familar and often quoted matter of record: canvas-back duck, hominy, madeira wine, and a chafing dish on the table to keep the food hot. After the meal, Washington stood on the steps of the larger building while the regiment passed in review. This dramatic event was re-enacted with carefully documented accuracy as a part of the opening of the Bicentennial Celebration in 1974. For a brief hour, time turned backward with intense credibility. The Tavern, once again crowded with distinguished guests of honor, was the center of hospitality and service.

Earlier, in 1787, the first in a series of birthday balls honoring Washington was held at Gadsby's. Later that year there was an elaborate ball given by the Light Infantry Company. Both of these events were held in the older and smaller of the buildings. The first large ball in the ballroom of the corner building was held in February 1793. It was rated a great success, to be followed by another ball to celebrate the Fourth of July. The events of the day began with service at Christ Church which was attended by President Washington, who was then beginning his second term in office, and an impressive roster of dignitaries, national and local. Then began a parade accompanied by the periodic booming of cannon fire and the bagpipes of the St. Andrew's Society. A banquet followed in the ballroom. The facilities of the new ice-house under the Tavern were sorely taxed that day, for every avail-

Musicians' balcony in the ballroom, entered by ladder from hallway.

Courtesy the curator, Gadsby's Tavern.

able choice viand was served to the guests. Fifteen rounds of toasts continued long into the evening. The last of these, made by Washington, was "Prosperity to the town of Alexandria." It was remembered and appropriately repeated by President James Madison when he was guest of honor at another banquet on May 9, 1809.

The last birthday celebration Washington attended in Alexandria was on February 11, 1799, the last year of his life. "Went up to Alexandria to the celebration of my birthday," he penned in his diary. "Many Manoeuvres were performed by the Uniform Corps, and an elegant Ball and Supper at Night." What a day! The celebration continued from dawn long into the night, with parading, artillery fire, open house at every tavern in the town, plus the ball and the banquet.

Gadsby's heyday was long gone as the old hostelry passed through a succession of owners and innkeepers in the years prior to and during the Civil War. In 1879 its doors were closed for lack of a tenant. Thereafter, for nearly a half-century the indignities to which the proud old building were submitted by economic necessity are best left unchronicled. The ripping out in 1917 of its front door, mantels and ballroom left it a sad derelict to neglect and deterioration. But that, too, is but one chapter in the story of Gadsby's Tavern. The Alexandria American Legion Post 24 purchased the building in 1929, unmindful at the time that the Great Depression lay just ahead. Renovation and restoration came slowly, but come they did, and the spirits of the old building began to revive. Old friends did, indeed, remember it.

As recently as 1943 the records of the Royal Arch Masons report that "on this evening (July 2) at the close of the Royal Arch Chapter, the entire membership repaired to Gadsby's Tavern where refreshments were served. The ghosts of our departed companions with that of our Most Worshipful George Washington must have attended that meeting."

Though Gadsby's was not operated as a tavern, there was life here once more. For a number of years the presentation of an eighteenth century theatrical revival by the Alexandria Little Theatre was held here, first in the ballroom and then in the courtyard.

Today, Gadsby's Tavern belongs to the City of Alexandria. It was purchased from American Legion Post 24 with certain provisions: the two buildings that comprise the Tavern are to be restored in "Williamsburg quality" by January 1976. A rear wing to the larger building which was added in 1878 is to be renovated by the City and occupied by the Legion Post in perpetuity.

The authentic restoration of the building in so far as much of its equipment goes, has been immeasurably aided by the necessary digging into its foundations. Artifacts that have been retrieved give valuable information about such specific details as the patterns of china and pottery that were in use, samples of glassware, wine bottles, cooking utensils, spoons, and a large variety of "the things guests leave behind," such as wig curlers, shoe buckles and button hooks.

What a great day for Alexandria when once again the hospitable doors of this great old center of entertainment swing open!

From Gadsby's Tavern, cross Royal Street to:

City Hall is open daily · Entrance to lobby where Alexandria artifacts are on display is through loggia from north side of Market Square · Underground parking · Frequent concerts in the Square.

Market Square in Alexandria has always been Market Square—the center of the town from the beginning. On that day in July, 1749, when the first lots were auctioned for a town yet to be built, two half-acre lots, No's 42 and 43, were set aside for the Town Hall and Market Place before the auctioning began. During the two and a quarter centuries since that day, the Square has undergone numerous changes. At one time so encroached upon by buildings that it was scarcely a Square at all, it is now more open than at any other time in its history.

There is only one building on Market Square today. This is the time-worn red brick City Hall, facing on three streets and occupying about half the block. A tall white stone tablet set into the wall of this building (on the Cameron Street side, just off Royal Street) gives the history of Market Square. Time and weather have worn the carved lettering nearly beyond reading, so a bronze marker nearby repeats the inscription. It is too long, the story too compact to be absorbed quickly on an always busy, often windy street corner. For your convenience we have reproduced it on page 68.

City Hall lacks the venerable age of some of its neighboring buildings, but it is an imposing red brick structure, completely Victorian in architecture. It is ornamented by the town clock, facing Royal Street, and decorated by rows of six-pointed star-shaped iron tie rods. It was built in 1873 on the site of several older buildings. Still safely vaulted in it is the priceless original minute book of the town trustees. The time-mottled pages spell out in clearly legible penmanship the plans that were discussed and the action taken during the early years of the town's history.

66

The clock in the steeple of City Hall still marks
the passing of time.

ALEXANDRIA, VIRGINIA
County seat of Fairfax 1742–1800
Organized 13 July 1749
Incorporated by the Assembly of Virginia 1779
Ceded to the Federal Government 1789
First boundary stone of the Federal District of Columbia
laid 15th of April 1791
Capitulated to the British 28th of August 1814
Retroceded to Virginia July 1846

The Market Square is the historic center of the town. In it the troops of Braddock were drilled 1755 and the news of his defeat at Ft. Duquesne was announced to the country 16th of July 1755.

The Carlyle House in Fairfax Street was the Headquarters of General Braddock during the French and Indian War, and was the scene of the council of Royal Governors Dinwiddie of Virginia, Shirley of Massachusetts, Delancy of New York, Morris of Pennsylvania and Sharp of Maryland, at which the first suggestion was made by British officials in council of taxing the American colonies. On this occasion Washington received his appointment as aide to General Braddock. Here also was held in 1785 a conference between the Governors of Virginia and Maryland which resulted in a convention of delegates from all the states at Philadelphia in 1787. This convention framed the Constitution of the United States.

In the Market Square stood the old Fairfax County Courthouse where the freeholders of the town and county assembled 18th of July 1771; at this meeting George Washington presided and George Mason drew up the celebrated Fairfax County Resolutions protesting against British tyranny. The County Courthouse was the point of beginning of the survey of the Federal District 1791. Here George Washington polled his last vote 1799 and his will was probated 10th of January 1800.

At the old City Tavern, corner of Royal and Cameron Streets, Washington had his headquarters as Colonel of the Virginia Militia when drilling his troops 1754. The first celebration of the adoption of the Federal Constitution was held at this Tavern 27th of June 1788 and from the doorway 16th of April 1789 General Washington on his way to his first inauguration responded to a farewell address made by Colonel Mayor Dennis Ramsay on behalf the citizens of Alexandria. From the hostelry General Washington issued his last military order when receiving the Independent Blues 1799.

Here is the entry of May 30, 1751: "It is thought necessary by the Trustees present that there be a meeting held in said town on the 2nd Saturday of every month in order to propose and put in execution such schemes as may be proposed for the benefit and advancement of the said Town, also that the clerk be ordered to attend."

On August 3, 1751, "Major John Carlyle is appointed to have a good road cleared down to Point Lumley (at the foot of Duke Street) and to see the streets kept in repair."

Legislation was enacted in 1752 that fairs were to be held in March and October of each year "for the sale and vending of all manner of cattle, victuals, provisions, wares and merchandise whatsoever." The legislation further provided that for those five days twice a year "persons coming to, being at, or going from the same, together with their cattle, goods, wares and merchandise will be exempt and privileged from all arrests, attachments etc. except for capital offenses, breaches of the peace or for any controversies, suits and quarrels that might arise and happen during the time."

Coincident with the legislation authorizing the semi-annual fairs was the practical matter of constructing a jail. It was a small building, erected about 1752, on a site indicated by a marker on the southwest corner of City Hall, on North Fairfax Street. Adjacent to it was a whipping post where occasional floggings attracted spectators. Among the jail's most notable occupants were prisoners taken during the French and Indian War.

The construction of the first Court House was also an important matter for trustee action. On December, 1752, the record shows, "It is ordered that John Carlyle, John Dalton, George Johnstone, William Ramsay view what is further necessary to be done to the finishing of the Court House and report the same on Saturday the 20th and that John Dalton be appointed overseer of the town in the room of John Carlyle, resigned."

The building of the court house was financed through a

An old white stone marker on City Hall records history, but with some inaccuracies.

Major John Carlyle is appointed to have a good road cleared
(From the old minutes book).

lottery, which was a generally accepted system for raising money, whether for public buildings or churches. Tickets were sold by the town trustees. The records do not show how many tickets were sold, but they do show, in one of the old ordinance books, that authorization was given for payment for a "treat" consisting of two and one-half gallons of rum and sugar.

Shortly after the erection of the Town Hall, the trustees authorized the erection at the foot of Duke Street on the point there of a warehouse. This building was 100 feet long, 24 feet wide, 13 feet pitched, and was paid for by the trustees. They also ordered that brick or stone chimneys be built to such houses and smith shops "as at present have wooden ones."

Merchants were eager to be as close as possible to the market place. The south side of King Street was considered to be the prime location for shops. In short time, every lot was occupied by some type of business . . . stores, offices, shops of artisans of many kinds. Public pumps were favorite gathering places, for water mains leading into the buildings were still years ahead, and the entire town depended upon wells and springs.

During the 25 years between the beginning of Alexandria and the outbreak of the Revolutionary War, Market Square was the center of dawn to dark activity. Construction was going on all around it. Ox-drawn carts were rutting the unpaved streets as they brought in loads of lumber and brick. News spread "on the wind" from downriver vantage points of the arrival of vessels from abroad. The docks were crowded with workmen unloading and reloading. Wagons jostled through the muddy, and if not muddy, dusty streets. They were loaded high with crates of frying-size chickens, geese and ducks, squealing young pigs and country-cured hams, baskets of cabbage and other vegetables and fruit, sides of freshly-killed beef, and wooden casks of cool butter and cheese. Work horses shared the hitching rails with impatient thoroughbreds whose riders had business in the court house or bank and the carriages of ladies intent on shopping. The air was always flavored with pitch and tar, wet sail-cloth and hempen rope, oakum, and fertilizer which was a by-product of the waterfront fishing industry and with which farmers loaded their empty wagons before returning home from a day in town.

The hard-used old Town House around which the life of the community centered was altered from time to time to meet growing needs. From about 1811 the building was shared with the Alexandria-Washington Masonic Lodge 22 whose museum housed a large collection of treasures associated particularly with Washington and Lafayette. On May 19, 1871, fire broke out in the building. While heroic efforts saved much that was valuable, the building itself was a smoldering ruin.

The City Hall of today was erected two years later in 1873. It included on the third floor, in the higher central portion on Cameron Street, new lodge rooms and facilities for several masonic groups. In the Council Chamber on the second floor, the present-day mayor and council members hold meetings on a raised platform in front of a large and handsome walnut-framed mural copied from an 1863 lithograph of the Alexandria waterfront. The original, done by Charles Magnus, of New York, is in the Mariners Museum, Newport News, Va. Two excellent oil portraits are on the walls of the Council Chamber: to the mayor's right, George Washington; to his left, Robert E. Lee.

From North Fairfax Street side of City Hall, cross the street to:

BANK OF ALEXANDRIA
Southeast corner of North Fairfax
and Cameron Streets

Closed for restoration.

The Bank of Alexandria occupies one of the choice lots in the oldest section of the town. Although it is scheduled for restoration and may not be open to the public for some time, it represents in its present condition an important transitional stage in the life of a valuable historic landmark. After long service as a bank, the handsome Federal style building has in more recent years housed a variety of shops and businesses. Vacant and boarded up now, it is in the safe custody of the Northern Virginia Park Authority, standing in line in a sense behind the neighboring Carlyle House awaiting its time for restoration. Visitors who have special interest in the construction of such an eighteenth century public building will be rewarded by seeing architectural details which are now exposed, but will no longer be visible when reconstruction has been completed.

By 1790 Alexandria was becoming such an important center of business in Northern Virginia that 130 citizens petitioned the General Assembly for a bank. The petition was granted, and the Bank of Alexandria became the first bank to be authorized in Virginia and the second one south of Philadelphia. The population was still small—no more than about 3,000—but the Alexandria waterfront was teeming with business. On a single day, December 12, 1792, the local newspaper reported the arrival of two ships each from London, Boston and Philadelphia, and the departure of six for Falmouth, Lisbon, Cadiz, Salem, Havre de Grace and New York.

The bank opened for business in a building at 305 Cameron Street. The capital was a maximum of $150,000, divided into 750 shares. As might well be expected, George Washington who, at this time was serving his second term as President of the United States, became a depositor and, from 1796 until his death, a shareholder.

The first president of the bank, from 1792 to 1796, was Philip Fendall, whose handsome house at 429 North Washington Street is open to visitors. He was succeeded by William Herbert, son-in-law of John Carlyle; and from that time to the present, the name Herbert has been prominently associated with the banking business in Alexandria. Under his administration, the splendid old building that continues to be identified as the Bank of Alexandria was constructed and, according to an old bill of sale, the building at 305 Cameron Street was sold.

The Bank has undergone numerous physical changes through the years; however, deep within the old walls is the original iron vault in which valuables were stored, behind a heavy disguising wooden door. This and other early architectural features will be preserved in the restoration program.

Walk south on North Fairfax Street to King Street, cross King Street and continue on South Fairfax Street to:

STABLER-LEADBEATER APOTHECARY SHOP
105 South Fairfax Street

Open daily 9 a.m. to 5 p.m. · Museum and antiques-gift shop · Maintained and operated by the Landmarks Society · No admission charge · Voluntary contributions accepted.

An apothecary shop, or drug store, in an old town is not apt to be the scene of events of great historic importance. The life of the town and its inhabitants is rather written from birth to death in the prescriptions that were filled, the various medications and supplies that were purchased, and the everyday coming and going of people.

The Stabler-Leadbeater Apothecary Shop in Alexandria served the community from 1792 until 1933. When it was closed, this was the oldest shop in Virginia and the second oldest in the United States in continuous operation. The chances are that during its 141 years of service, nearly every man, woman and child who lived in Alexandria came into the shop on one occasion or another. George Washington picked up his mail here and Mrs. Washington wrote her request to Mr. Stabler for "a quart of his best Castor Oil and the bill for it."

During the period when Alexandria was a part of the

Glimpse through the bow front window into the Stabler-Leadbeater Apothecary Shop.

District of Columbia, three senators among the five who were named as recently as 1957 by a special committee of the U.S. Senate to the Senate Hall of Fame, were frequent visitors to the Apothecary Shop; and when Daniel Webster, from Massachusetts; Henry Clay, from Kentucky; and John C. Calhoun, from South Carolina chanced to meet here and became engaged in conversation, bystanders were treated to a choice opportunity to hear the topics of disagreement of the day oratorically aired.

When the shop was closed, it was purchased by a group of interested women in the community organized as the Landmarks Society. The building has been maintained so well under the care of this group that it seems to have been scarcely touched by the passing of the years. Except for some slight changes such as the two front windows which, even so, conform to the old shutters which are still in the shop, everything is so nearly as it always was that eighteenth century Alexandrians would feel quite at home in it. If Mr. Leadbeater is not in sight in the shop, he probably is behind the high counter. The story of the Apothecary Shop that visitors hear by tape recording might well be his own.

High on the rear wall in sight of everyone who enters is the large, easily read clock which goes back to the 1790s. When it was new, the clock had wooden works and is reputed to have kept excellent time. But the old wooden works gave way to a new set of brass works and the old clock continued to tick away the hours. Yes, it is still capable of running, but only for a brief period. Then it stops to rest awhile.

In place on the shelves and in glass cases is the largest and most valuable collection of medicinal glass in the country. The various types and sizes of the glass bottles merit more than a casual glance. Here are hundreds of hand-blown bottles, many with genuine gold-leaf labels. There are curious hook-necked bottles made in Bottomsworth, England, and transported in sailing vessels; croton oil bottles produced in Alexandria; opodeldoc bottles which contained a popular camphorated soap liniment; glass nursing bottles for babies who used cloth stoppers for nipples; and the bright blue containers reserved for poisons. Some of the very small bottles were designed by the first owner of the shop and made in Alexandria according to his directions.

On the counter where prescriptions were carefully mixed, there are two tiles which were used for mixing powders. On one, the medication was prepared for humans; on the other for animals. Horses particularly were an essential part of the in-town service as they provided transportation and their care was important to the economy.

Behind the counter along the south wall are ranks of mahogany drawers, each with a porcelain handle, probably imported from England. Many of these handles bear the names of the contents to be found in the various drawers.

The large glass globes of colored water in the front windows are traditional symbols of an apothecary shop, used in the beginning as a means of identification for illiterate persons. Legend is that in many communities in times of epidemics and plagues, both globes were filled with red liquid as a sign to visitors not to stop in the town. This would have been the case in Alexandria particularly in 1803 and again in 1807 when there were plagues of cholera and yellow fever. Located as the town was on a busy waterfront to which came sailors and visitors from all the ports of the world, the town fathers were well aware both of the constant need for caution in protecting the residents and of the value to them of a good apothecary shop. Under the direction of Dr. Elisha Cullen Dick, first Alexandria health officer, strict rules were enforced whenever he considered these necessary.

Today the red and green globes are no more than symbols from another day to remind you of a friendly visit to an historic shop.

Walk south on South Fairfax Street to Prince Street. Turn left one block to:

THE ATHENAEUM
201 Prince Street

Open 10 a.m. to 4 p.m. Tuesday through Saturday, 1 to 4 p.m. Sunday. Closed on Monday.

The Athenaeum, like the Lyceum, is also a Greek revival building, unusual in Alexandria. It was erected in the mid-nineteenth century, designed and planned to serve as a banking house for the Bank of the Old Dominion. The bank continued in operation here until Alexandria was occupied by Union forces at the outbreak of the Civil War. First blood was shed in the Marshall House, a tavern on King Street, now long gone, when the innkeeper shot and killed Colonel Elmer Ellsworth, of the New York Zouave regiment which had just landed by boat at the foot of King Street. The Colonel had ripped from its flagpole the large Confederate flag. As a result of this action, tempers ran high, fear filled the air, and the threat of mob violence hung like a fog over the town.

Stand here, if you will, in front of this lovely old building, serene behind its classic columns, painted to harmonize with the marigolds of summer and the foliage of autumn. Watch for a moment. Darkness has settled at last upon the old town at the end of a day of bloody violence. The question is in every mind, on every tongue; "What will the morning bring?"

To one quiet, courteous, mild-mannered man named William Henry Lambert, there is a special anxiety. What will happen to the assets of the Bank of the Old Dominion, of which he is the cashier? Events have moved so rapidly that no plans have been made to move them. Dare he run the risk at this late date of trying to get them to a place of safety if, indeed, such a place can be found? After a quick and guarded consultation with his president, Robert H. Miller, Lambert goes into action.

Shambling through the shadows along the side street moves

a nondescript old wagon, easily lost in the darkness as it comes to a standstill near the rear door. The cashier can find his way without a glimmer of lantern to the vaults that hold the assets and important papers entrusted to the bank for safe-keeping. The wagon creeps along again with its precious burden to a designated spot. Who knows where? The two responsible bank officials kept their counsel to the end. When peace came, the assets of the Bank of the Old Dominion were retrieved intact. It was the only state bank in Virginia to redeem its outstanding currency dollar for dollar. But the bank never opened again except as it was amalgamated into larger banking facilities of the postwar era.

For a long time, the building served as a Free Methodist Church. Then, as it was left untenanted, grime collected on the columns, spiders spun their soot-snaring webs, and debris was whirled into the corners of the portico.

A new life began in 1964 when the building was acquired as the permanent home of the Northern Virginia Fine Arts Association. Completely renovated and adapted to new requirements, the building is now known by its classical name, the Athenaeum. It is host to a succession of art exhibits, displays of arts and crafts, and offers a varied program of services and activities.

Houses Associated with Historic Personages and Events

THERE is not one building or early section of a building in old Alexandria, it is safe to say, that was not at one time or another associated with distinguished personages and events. In the shops of merchants and craftsmen, men like George Washington and George Mason and Robert E. Lee ordered their homeliest necessities, exchanged greetings with friends and neighbors, talked about the day's news. They owned tenant houses and offices and servants quarters which they planned and managed. They had business at the bank, the town hall, the taverns. They visited in the homes of friends. Alexandria was their home town.

The houses you will visit on this tour are fourteen in number, each with a special and different interest, the houses in which the leaders who were "bone-and-blood" of the town made their homes and reared their families.

Among the leading families of Old Alexandria and the nearby estates in Northern Virginia there was so much inter-

81

Dr. William Brown bought this white clapboard and brick house in 1783.

marrying that the family trees have become as pleached as are the beeches in the formal gardens at Colonial Williamsburg. Second and third marriages often followed death in child birth of young wives; and several children of the same father, with the same family names, were both half brothers and sisters and several grades of cousins and cousins removed.

Genealogical records for such families as the Alexanders, Fairfaxes, Washingtons, Lees and others are available in the Virginia Room of Alexandria Library, 717 Queen Street.

The houses you will see were built during the first 65 to 70 years after the founding of Alexandria (1749–1820). Although they vary widely in size and style, each reflecting the background, tastes and family requirements of the first owners, all show careful architectural design and planning combined with sound construction. With the exception of Carlyle House, all are built flush with the sidewalk; and several are closely neighbored by comparable residences of the same period. The prevailing architecture is mid-Georgian, although the wider doorways and side lights in some of the houses indicate a growing popularity for the Federal style.

Most of the buildings have undergone numerous changes through the years. Such Victorian additions as porches and *porte-cochères* which were made in the latter part of the nineteenth century have been removed to restore the buildings to their original appearance.

This Tour follows a geographical route. It begins at Ramsay House, oldest house in Alexandria, which now serves as a Visitors Center and headquarters of the Alexandria Tourist Council, 221 King Street, and concludes near the Bicentennial Center, 201 South Washington Street. The Lee-Fendall House and the Fitzhugh-Lee House are open as house museums and gift shops. A small admission charge is made. The Lloyd House is being prepared to serve public purposes and is open. The other houses are private residences some of which are open to visitors on special occasions.

Ramsay House, showing the oldest section at the right that came to town on a barge.

RAMSAY HOUSE
221 King Street

Home of William Ramsay · Open daily 10 a.m. to 4:30 p.m. · Oldest house in Alexandria · Visitors Center · Permits for free parking in metered spaces available upon request to out of town visitors · 13-minute movie, "Alexandria, Va.—George Washington's Home Town" shown twice daily and by special request · Lists of restaurants and shops in Old Town · Guided tours can be arranged for groups with special interests · Information about special events and activities · No admission or other charge.

The first house in Alexandria, now its oldest building and still anchored firmly on a heavy stone foundation, arrived just as did many of the early settlers and most of their possessions —at a wharf near the foot of King Street. This is the Ramsay House, headquarters of the Alexandria Tourist Council.

_he *entire* white clapboard house as it appears today did
not, of course, come sailing up the Potomac River. It was only
the small, oldest portion, which is now used as an office; and
there is historic precedent for this continuing use of it.

William Ramsay, an energetic, enterprising young Scotsman, member of a prominent Scottish family and well-con-
nected in Virginia, arrived in the colonies in the 1740s. He
lived for a time at Dumfries, not far down the Potomac, where
he represented a firm of Glasgow merchants. He was soon
engaged in some mercantile ventures with a fellow Scotsman,
John Carlyle, in the small warehouse settlement of Belhaven.
Both were among the first eleven trustees of Alexandria and
both bought lots at the first auction, July 13, 1749. Ramsay
was so eager to get into business on his own property that he
is reliably believed to have loaded a small building on a barge,
towed it up to Alexandria, and settled it on one of the two
lots he had purchased. Before his fellow-trustees and other
property owners could arrange for timber and bricks, young
Ramsay had a roof over his head and a combination residence-
business office. His entire business career in Alexandria which
continued through the Revolutionary War, until his death in
1795, indicates that this action was completely characteristic
of the man.

As his business and his family grew, William Ramsay
erected other buildings on adjacent lots, some of which he
purchased when these were forfeited by the original owners
for lack of compliance with the building regulations. But the
first house remained in service for a variety of uses through
three generations. Clement E. Conger, distinguished nationally
as a curator, and a direct descendant of William Ramsay, says
that during the Revolutionary War period, the lawn in front
of the house extended one block eastward to the Potomac
River and was adorned by beautiful trees. Old pictures of the
house show doors opening directly onto North Fairfax and
King streets, and an outside staircase leading to the main floor.

In addition to his numerous thriving and profitable mercantile enterprises, William Ramsay served his community well as town overseer, census taker, postmaster and member of the Committee of Safety. As a part of the observance of St. Andrew's Day in 1761, this distinguished Scotsman, recognized by the members of the St. Andrew's Society as "first projector and founder of this promising city," was designated as Lord Mayor of Alexandria and invested with a gold chain and medal.

When the newly-appointed Commander-in-Chief of the Continental Army came through Alexandria on May 5, 1775 on his way from Mount Vernon to Philadelphia where he was to accept command, General Washington had breakfast in this house with his long-time friends, the William Ramsays. Mrs. Ramsay was as tireless in her support of the fight for freedom as was her husband. This gallant lady, on her own, collected the sum of $75,812—a remarkably large amount at the time—to promote the war effort. Twenty years after this visit, when the Revolutionary War had been won and the Constitution of the United States adopted, George Washington, who had retired to a quiet life at Mount Vernon after eight years of the presidency, wrote this in his diary: "Received an Invitation to the Funeral of Willm. Ramsay, Esqr, of Alexandria, the oldest Inhabitt. of the Town; and went up."

The eldest Ramsay son, Colonel Dennis Ramsay, who was born in this house in 1756, also became one of the foremost citizens of Alexandria. He was elected mayor in 1789, and it was in this capacity that he is believed to be the first official to address General Washington as "Mr. President." This the mayor did at a celebration honoring Washington on his way to New York for his first inauguration on April 30, 1789. The third generation of Ramsays associated with the old house was named, not surprisingly, George Washington Dennis Ramsay.

The Ramsay House as it appears today between two massive chimneys that seem somewhat like book-ends is still a small white clapboard building with a Dutch roof and three dormer windows overlooking North Fairfax Street and Market Square. It is removed two blocks from the riverfront, long ago filled in to provide more building space, but is still aproned from its front porch by a perpetually green and fragrant garden where you may pause to rest.

When preparations were being made for the 200th observance of the founding of Alexandria, in 1949, the Ramsay House was in such a sad state of dilapidation that it was near collapse. Efforts to save the building culminated in its purchase by the City of Alexandria. It was rehabilitated under the direction of a restoration architect and fittingly furnished for its present continuing service.

Walk north on Fairfax Street to the Center of the block to:

THE CARLYLE HOUSE
Center of 100 block, North Fairfax Street

Closed for restoration 1975–76. Visitors may see the reconstruction under way.

The mansion on North Fairfax Street facing Market Square was built in 1752 by John Carlyle. It has two claims to interest. Architecturally it is regarded as one of the great eighteenth century houses of Virginia. Historically, in this house in colonial times events took place that affected the destiny of the United States as a nation. It has been called appropriately the "real birthplace" of the American Revolution. Now the property of the Northern Virginia Park Authority, the building is being restored to its original appearance and elegance and will be open to the public.

John Carlyle came to Virginia as a young man about 1740 from Dumfries, Scotland, a center of turbulence during the border wars between England and Scotland. He settled first at

The Carlyle House will be the center of an historic park.

Courtesy the Northern Virginia Regional Park Authority.

Dumfries on the Potomac where he represented one of the large Glasgow firms engaging in business with the colonists. In partnership with John Dalton, he had numerous interests in the vicinity prior to the founding of Alexandria and was one of the first trustees. He had married Sara Fairfax, daughter of Colonel William Fairfax, of Belvoir Manor, and for her he planned the handsome mansion, built on the third lot put up for auction July 13, 1749, and an additional lot he bought from William Ramsay. Unlike other eighteenth century residences in Alexandria, the Carlyle House was built more in the style of such manor houses as Gunston Hall and Mount Vernon, with several dependencies apart from the main building. The regulation of the town trustees that dwelling houses must be built in line with the street was formulated at the time the Carlyle House was under construction and did not apply to it.

John Carlyle's mansion, built in 1752, under reconstruction.

That the house was built in 1752 is attested by the keystone over the front doorway which bears the date and also the names of the owners. Carlyle was a ship owner, among his other business enterprises, and was able to bring directly to Alexandria in his own ships the best furniture and furnishings available in England. Through his wife's Fairfax connections, this Scottish merchant was also appointed in 1758 to serve as Collector of His Majesty's customs at the Port of Alexandria. He also served as manager of Mason's Ordinary, the small inn that became a part of Gadsby's Tavern. From about 1761 to the outbreak of the Revolution this Ordinary was owned by John Carlyle and John Dalton.

The threat to colonial peace during the 1750s and into the 1760s was the encroachment from Canada of the French in alliance with the Indians in the Ohio valley. As a result of this, Major General Edward Braddock was sent from England with a contingent of regular troops to "deal with the trouble" in an efficient military manner. Alexandria shortly became one of the focal points from which his attacks upon the enemy would be launched. "It was like a garrisoned town," according to an old report, "teeming with troops, and resounding with the drum and fife." A brilliant campaign was about to open under the auspices of an experienced general, and with all the means and appurtenances of European warfare. Every day in Market Square there was the sound of marching feet as the militia drilled under the leadership of young Major George Washington.

General Braddock, who made his headquarters in the Carlyle House, used the handsome mansion for a conference with a group of colonial governors to consider the increasingly serious problem and plan a course of military action. This conference was held April 14, 1755, attended by Governors Dinwiddie of Virginia, Shirley of Massachusetts, Sharpe of Maryland, Morris of Pennsylvania and Delancey of New York.

One result of the Carlyle House Conference was a dispatch General Braddock sent to London. He wrote: "I cannot but take the liberty to represent to you the necessity of *laying a tax* upon all his Majesty's dominions in America . . . for reimbursing the great sums that must be advanced for the service and interest of the colonies in this important crisis." This advise was implemented a decade later in the form of the hated Stamp Act. Thus it was that the fuse that was lit in 1755 at Carlyle House in Alexandria ultimately resulted in the explosion in 1776 at Lexington and Concord.

Another result of the conference was that George Washington, who had just turned 23, made so favorable an impression on the company that he was quickly caught up in the excitement of military leadership. A small leather-bound biographical memoir of Washington compiled shortly after his death provides a vivid account of what followed this conference: "As in consequence of a military Regulation, 'no Officer who did not derive his Commission from the King could command one who did,' Washington resigned (as an officer in the Virginia Militia); but strongly attached to the military Life, and emulous to defend his Country with distinguished Zeal, he voluntarily served under General Braddock as an extra Aid-Decamp to General Braddock. That General marched against Fort Du Quesne; but soon after he crossed the River Monongahela, the van Division of his Army was attacked by an ambuscade of French and Indians, and totally defeated.—The thickness of the woods prevented both the Europeans and provincial Troops from being able to defend themselves with effect; they could neither keep their Ranks, nor charge the Enemy with the Bayonet, while the Indians, who were expert at bush fighting, and were widely scattered, fired at them in all directions from behind the Trees where they were concealed from their Foes, and took a fatal Aim. Washington had cautioned General Braddock in vain; his ardent desire for conquest made him deaf to the voice of prudence; he saw his Error when too late, and bravely perished in his endeavors to save the Division from Destruction. The Gallant but Unfortunate General had four horses shot from under him before he was slain, and almost every Officer whose Duty obligated him to be on Horseback, was either killed or wounded except Washington."

The lessons learned under such tragic circumstances would, at a later day, be the basis for the successful strategy enabling Washington's soldiers to crush the British regulars at the Battle of Kings Mountain, thus turning the tide of the American Revolution toward victory.

Visitors resting on a bench in Alexandria's Market Square and looking across the street at the old Carlyle House may marvel that so much could have started here.

John Carlyle died in 1780 and was buried in the Old Presbyterian Cemetery nearby. His only son was killed the following year at the Battle of Eutaw Springs, serving in the cavalry under General "Lighthorse Harry" Lee. Even so, the house continued to serve as a center of political and social activities for many years. Among the distinguished guests who enjoyed its hospitality were: Benjamin Franklin, the Marquis de Lafayette, General Lee, George Mason, John Marshall, Thomas Jefferson, Charles Carroll and John Paul Jones.

When they knew the mansion, the entrance facade, facing Fairfax Street, had a handsome gate leading to a flagged terrace with a retaining wall. In addition to the main house, there were two wings which were destroyed long ago. On the east, the property fell away sharply to the river which, at that time, came up to what is now Lee Street. The house was remodeled in the Federal manner in 1820. The entrance door, stairway, window trim and most of the mantels were changed. A Victorian veranda was added across the rear when another style of architecture became popular. From that time until recently, the old house was hidden from view behind a commercial building erected directly in front of it. While it was maintained as a museum and the famous Blue Room and a small adjoining library remained untouched, many Alexandrians walking within a few feet of the historic old house, were scarcely aware of its existence.

This historic property is now owned by the Northern Virginia Regional Park Authority. Its restoration is being carried out with financial help from the Historic Preservation Project of the U.S. Department of Housing and Urban Development. When the house is once again open to the public, it will resemble as nearly as possible the mid-eighteenth century mansion in which John and Sara Carlyle lived and reared their children. The furnishings will include some furniture, paintings and other personal possessions of the Carlyle family.

Walk south across King Street to:

DR. WILLIAM BROWN HOUSE
212 South Fairfax Street

Private residence.

The faintly discernible inscription on a time worn stone in the graveyard of Pohick Episcopal Church south of Alexandria on Jefferson Davis Highway is fitting introduction to the doctor whose name is associated with this house. It reads

in part: "In memory of William Brown, M.D., Physician General to the Hospitals of the United States, who died on the 11th day of January, 1792, in the 44th year of his age. His benevolence, curtesy and integrity as a man secured him the applause of his country, the honor and emoluments of his Profession, the respect of the Wealthy and the veneration of the poor."

In common with many other early leaders of Alexandria, he was a Scotsman, born in 1748 and educated at the University of Edinburgh. He embarked shortly after graduation for Virginia where he found hospitality among Scottish friends and relatives in Dumfries and at Rippon Lodge and, in the spring of 1772, a welcome from George Washington at Mount Vernon. He also found a wife with whom he settled for a brief time in the house on Cameron Street that Washington referred to often as "my small house in town." The modest rent he paid was cancelled, according to Washington's records, "for professional services."

The respect Washington felt for this Scottish doctor sixteen years his junior is revealed in the appointment, at the outbreak of the Revolutionary War, of Dr. William Brown to serve as Physician-General and Director of Hospitals of the Continental Army, a combined post which he held for two years. He not only served throughout the long war but prepared and, in 1778, published the first American *Pharmacopeia*.

After the war, in 1783, Dr. Brown purchased this house. Unfortunately other builders of early residences did not follow the lead of John Carlyle who had his and his wife's names and the date of their home carved over the front door. Even so, while deeds and construction records are not available for some of the earliest houses, the buildings speak with remarkable definity of their own age. This house, for instance, in the center of the oldest section of Alexandria, is obviously of early construction. While the house appears to be of clapboard, it is actually of solid brick, two and a half stories, with the clapboards serving as sheathing. The interior walls, underneath

The eighteenth century kitchen continues to be functional.

present-day plastering, are also of solid brick. In contrast to some of the large brick mid-Georgian houses erected at a later time, Dr. Brown's house, with its neat front porch and simple doorway has an almost provincial air; however, the interior woodwork, most of which is original and has been well preserved, is rated among the best in town.

The "service facilities" that have survived in this house give a remarkably clear insight into housekeeping in an earlier day. In the kitchen the big fireplace has a Dutch oven built into the chimney and a heavy crane for suspending iron pots and kettles above the coals. A heavy hand-hewn stone sink with copper cauldron, complete with firebox, provided hot water for the kitchen and for an old wooden bathtub in a room adjoining the kitchen. In the service yard to the rear of the house are remnants, at least, of some of the outbuildings.

The hardships Dr. Brown underwent during the War, particularly in that bitter winter at Valley Forge, took early toll of his health. He died in January, 1792, age 44, after "a tedious and excruciating illness," according to the newspaper account, and was buried on the estate of his sister, Mrs. Charles Alexander, at Preston. Years later when the rails and wheels of progress (the Potomac Yards of the Southern Railway) invaded the riverside family graveyard, the remains of the doctor were removed to Pohick Church graveyard where the old marker stands.

This house which, after nearly two hundred years still bears his name, is one of the few in old Alexandria that, so far as records and physical evidence show, was never abandoned even for a season to the ravages of time, neglect and decay. It was sold in 1842 to a cabinet maker, James Green, whose fine furniture graced many houses of his day and is much in demand today.

Dr. William Brown was a relative of Dr. Gustavus Brown, of Port Tobacco, Maryland, who was one of the three physicians attending George Washington in his final illness.

Walk south one half block to Duke Street and turn left to:

The garden is beautiful at any season.

DR. JAMES CRAIK HOUSE
210 Duke Street

Private residence.

In this commodious four-story eighteenth century brick house a Scottish-born doctor and his wife reared their family of six sons and three daughters. He was an interesting man to know, Dr. James Craik.

Alexandria was still mostly unsettled woods and marshland when he was born in Scotland, in an area where the turbulence of border clashes between the Scotch and English was recent history. He came to Virginia via the West Indies about 1750, settling well back from tidewater country, in Winchester. There was turbulence here, too, as the French, moving aggressively south from Canada, stirred the Indians to hostility against the colonists in an effort to gain dominion over the English. Soon the young doctor volunteered to serve as surgeon in a locally-recruited regiment to join in the concerted attack against the marauders. So it was, at a hastily constructed wilderness palisade called Fort Necessity, after the colonel of his regiment had been killed in action, that Dr. James Craik met his new commander, Major George Washington.

One result of this meeting was that the Scottish doctor came in time to make his home in Alexandria and to spend the better part of a long life prominently associated with the early history of the old town.

The attack against the French and Indians had been carefully planned at a conference of colonial governors in nearby Carlyle House. It was led by General Braddock who had recently been sent from England with a company of Irish regulars which would be augmented by companies of colonial militia. The campaign turned into a rout as General Braddock's red coats, trained in conventional European warfare, proved no match for the guerrilla fighting they encountered in the Virginia wilderness. There, in the darkness of night and

96

Dr. James Craik, Washington's "compatriot in arms," lived in this commodious house.

bitter defeat, on the bank of the Monongahela, two young men upon whom heavy leadership responsibilities had fallen that day kept the death watch for General Braddock. Dr. Craik dressed the wounds of the dying leader. Major Washington read the simple burial service as companions kept wary guard.

The ties of friendship and mutual trust born on that bloody field would reach into this house and would affect the lives of its occupants for long years to come. The two men would be, in Washington's words, compatriots in arms throughout the American Revolution, in which Dr. Craik served when he was called upon as Chief Physician and Surgeon of the Continental Army, and was in charge of the hospital at Yorktown.

Dr. Craik's house, like most eighteenth century residences in Alexandria, is narrow in width, with only a handsome recessed entrance portico, one window, and a tall iron-grilled gate facing directly on the street. The house extends deep into a brick-walled garden onto which windows and doors open, and there are two full floors of bedrooms with more behind the dormer windows of the top floor. Like most old houses, this one has undergone alterations through the years, but without changing its appearance. The flounder house to the left was once a frame building with wood siding, later faced with brick.

The Craiks were a popular couple. With their large family, hospitality abounded in the old house. Growing boys scaled the trees in the garden and pretty girls were courted. Fires blazed merrily in every room on winter nights. On summer evenings guests found their way through the narrow brick passageway into the fragrance of the garden. Washington was often among the guests here as was Dr. Craik at Mount Vernon, sometimes with his family for social occasions, at other times as physician.

A few excerpts from Washington's diary during the last months of his life indicate the close relationship that had continued through so many years:

Dr. Craik and Dr. Gustavus Brown kept the death watch.

Courtesy The Corcoran Gallery of Art, Washington.

September 6, 1799—Dr. Craik sent for in the night to Mrs. Washington....

September 29—Dr. Craik came and stayed all night ...

November 27—Dr. Craik was sent for to Mrs. Lewis (Nellie Custis) who delivered her of a daughter ...

And then came the hurried pounding on the door of this house very early on a cold Saturday morning in December, 1799. Overnight, General Washington had, himself, become very ill. Dr. Gustavus Brown, from Port Tobacco, across the river, had also been summoned by Tobias Lear, Washington's secretary, and Dr. Craik quickly sent for Dr. Elisha Cullen Dick. Although Washington's illness was of brief duration—scarcely more than 24 hours—he seemed to know he was dying. The faithful secretary, mindful of an obligation to posterity, sat in the room with the anxious Martha, his pen ready to catch every word from the dying man. Thus we know that Washington said to Dr. Craik, "Doctor, I die hard, but I am not afraid to go. I believed from my first attack that I should not survive it. My breath cannot last long." Throughout the grey December day as snow lay in cold patches upon the grounds of Mount Vernon, the three doctors waged a losing battle for the life of George Washington. Dr. Craik gently comforted and ministered to the grieving Martha, not well herself at the time, and then sadly drove home where he wrote: "I kissed the cold hand which I held in my bosom, laid it down, and for some time was lost in profound grief."

Among the bequests made by Washington was a desk and chair to Dr. Craik. These he used in this house for a long time until old age forced his retirement to his country home, Vaucleuse. That property, on what is now Seminary Road, is well within the confines of Alexandria and is a part of the large tract on which the Alexandria Hospital and School of Nursing are located. Dr. Craik would surely have approved of this use for his country retreat.

After 84 useful years, he came to rest in the graveyard of the Old Presbyterian Meeting House.

Old houses are brick and stone, timbers and mortar, window-frames and doors . . . buildings in which people live. Only as the people who have lived in an old house come to life, themselves, long after they have gone, does one particular house as 210 Duke Street acquire a special personality of its own.

Walk east on Duke Street (toward the river) to South Lee Street and turn right to:

SNOWDEN HOUSE
611 South Lee Street

Private residence.

The Snowden House takes its name from the prominent Alexandria family of newspaper owners and editors who lived here for nearly a century. More recently, it was the home of

Supreme Court Justice Hugo L. Black who, shortly before his death, was memorably interviewed for television in his well-stocked library by Eric Sevareid. The distinguished jurist was a familiar figure on his tennis court well into his late years.

Samuel Snowden, the first member of the family to come to Alexandria, was born in New Jersey the year in which the Declaration of Independence was signed. He came to Virginia as a young man and in 1800, became owner and editor of Alexandria's newspaper, founded in 1784, and known through most of its long history as the *Alexandria Gazette*. The files of this newspaper, believed to be the oldest daily in continuous operation in the United States, are a priceless source of information about everything that went on in the old town, from wars and enemy occupation and fires and plagues, births, obituaries and fulsome eulogies to balls, parades, editorial opinions on every current matter of interest, and all the trivial that is so important in reconstructing the life of earlier days. These files are now on microfilm and are available to the public at the Alexandria Library, 717 Queen Street. They make fascinating and illuminating reading.

The house was built on "Alexander land" during the 1790s and, according to a deed granted in 1798, was leased by William Thornton Alexander "with house, buildings etc" to Thomas Vowell, Jr., who later purchased it. The architectural details of the exterior woodwork are notable. Your attention is directed to the formal doorway which gives access to a long hall on the north side of the house, to the details above the 24-paned windows facing the street, and to the beautifully carved cornice below the two dormer windows. There was at one time a "widow's" or "captain's walk" atop the mansion which provided a magnificent view of the Potomac River.

Among the buildings mentioned in the first recorded deed was a kitchen which was completely separate from the main house, as was often the case with other old houses of the period. A view from the garden side shows clearly where the service ell was in time joined to the residence.

Edgar Snowden, who succeeded his father as owner and editor of the *Gazette* bought the property in 1839, the year in which he was elected mayor of Alexandria. By this time, the newspaper had its own flag on which the pen appropriately rested upon the sword, and was as much a part of the community as were the people it served and the houses in which they lived. The Snowden House was occupied by successive generations of the family until well into the present century.

Walk north on South Lee Street to Duke Street, turn left on Duke Street to South St. Asaph Street (four blocks) to:

LAFAYETTE HOUSE
301 South St. Asaph Street

Private residence.

This handsome three-story brick Federal-style mansion has been known for the past 150 years as the Lafayette House although it was built about 1815 by Thomas Lawrason, a prosperous and prominent partner in a shipping firm, and has always been a private residence.

It became the Lafayette House in October of 1824 when the President of the United States borrowed it briefly, in the sense that the State Department makes arrangements for the housing of official visitors, to serve as Blair House in Washington does today, for the entertainment of the new nation's distinguished guest from France.

President James Monroe, toward the end of his second administration, had invited the Marquis de Lafayette to make an official visit. He was unlike many foreign visitors who come these days exhanging policies, negotiating treaties and seeking material aid; for this French nobleman had loved liberty and

Lafayette was lodged in this house on his official visit to the United States in 1824.

freedom enough, nearly a half-century earlier, to risk as much in its behalf as did any American patriot. The purpose in inviting him to return was to express to Lafayette the formal appreciation and gratitude of a people slowly recovering from a second war with England that had resulted in the burning of the Capitol.

To Alexandria, the anticipated visit was far more personal than would be the case in most of the cities on the official itinerary; for the old town and the French Marquis were old friends, familiar with the ways of each other. Thomas Lawrason had died in 1819; however, his house was the finest of the then new residences in Alexandria which, at the time, was a part of the Distirct of Columbia. His widow and children needed no urging in making it available.

In appreciation for this generosity, city officials instructed William A. Williams, an Alexandria silversmith, to design and make a handsome silver cup which was presented to Mrs. Lawrason.

As the Marquis was escorted into the high-ceilinged hall with its beautiful arch and graceful curving stairway, he must have had long thoughts . . . of his first visit to Alexandria when, as a very young man in a strange country, knowing little English, he arrived at Gadsby's Tavern on his way to Philadelphia to volunteer for service in the American fight for freedom . . . of that same young French nobleman, a newly-commissioned officer in the Continental Army, returning to Alexandria to take command of the Virginia light troops. He surely thought of Dr. James Craik whose house was a few doors down Duke Street and who had so gently dressed the Marquis' wounds at the Battle of Brandywine. And there was the day in 1781 when he came proudly into town at the head of an American army, on his way down the Potomac Path toward Yorktown. How helpfully the people of Alexandria responded when the wagons, supplies and horses he had requested had not yet arrived.

From this house, the Marquis would go by carriage down

to Woodlawn Plantation. There he would present to Nellie Custis Lewis, grand-daughter of his oftimes hostess at Mount Vernon, Martha Washington, his respects and an oil portrait of himself. He would call upon the widow of his old comrade-in-arms, General "Lighthorse Harry" Lee, who was living quietly with her children in an old house on Oronoco Street. Over teacups in her drawing room, he would inquire about young Robert E. Lee, who was preparing for West Point, and would brush off Mrs. Lee's concern for his five years of imprisonment during the French Revolution. Alors! Many of his friends had lost their heads to the guillotine.

Then back once more at Gadsby's Tavern, so familiar to him from so many visits, he would be guest of honor at a banquet. Another distinguished guest on that occasion was John Quincy Adams, then Secretary of State.

Leaving Alexandria at the end of this visit, the Marquis de Lafayette must surely have recalled another departure when George Washington had accompanied him to a waiting ship in Annapolis, and had then returned to Mount Vernon to write him thus: "I often asked myself, as our carriages separated, whether that was the last I ever should have seen of you."

Some years ago the great-great-grandson of the Marquis, on a visit to this country, came to Alexandria and was himself a guest in this house. At the front door, beneath the keystoned arch with its semi-circle of stars, which may or may not intentionally represent the thirteen original colonies, the past and the present met for the Comte de Lafayette. So they can for you.

The old mansion today, with its freshly painted doorway and well tended side garden, is a part of Alexandria's past *and* its present. A former owner—and the house has had many distinguished owners—often said, "I hold title to this house and am privileged to live in it; but in its historic association for a brief time with a great personage, it belongs to us all."

Walk across Duke Street to:

DULANY HOUSE
601 Duke Street

Private residence.

Benjamin Tasker Dulany (1754–1816) was a third-generation Irish American, son of a distinguished Maryland barrister, who loved good living and was amply able to provide it for himself and his family.

George Washington, himself, took credit for making a match between him and his bride who was a ward jointly of Washington and George Mason. He describes his part thus: "Our celebrated Miss French, whom half the world was in pursuit of, bestowed her hand on Wednesday last, being her birthday (you perceive I think myself under the necessity of accounting for her choice) upon Mr. Ben Dulany . . ." This was in February, 1773. The Dulanys moved from Maryland with their growing family before the Revolution and settled in a house on Shuter's Hill. There he bred and stabled fine horses on which he often "parted the wind" of the countryside. He was an expansive host and affectionate father.

He built this town house—possibly the finest example of Georgian architecture in Alexandria—in 1783 and continued to use it until 1810 when he sold it to Robert I. Taylor. During the period of his occupancy, Taylor was one of the prominent vestrymen of St. Paul's Episcopal Church, then being designed by Benjamin Latrobe, architect of the National Capitol. There is some reason to believe that the architect may, at least, have made some suggestions about the wing which Taylor added to connect the main house with the kitchen.

Imposing as is the exterior of this grey-painted brick house, it scarcely suggests the perfection of the interior. The architecture, furniture and furnishings, knowledgeably acquired by the present owners, compliment each other to produce a museum quality distinction.

When the Marquis de Lafayette with his entourage was

107

Dulany House, fine example of Georgian architecture, built in 1783.

housed across Duke Street in the residence of Mrs. Thomas Lawrason in October, 1824, neighbors and townspeople crowded the streets in enthusiastic welcome to a great hero. He came out to greet them from the front steps, but was quickly escorted across the street and to the higher entrance to this house.

Standing in front of the Dulany House today, you may easily imagine yourself a part of the eager crowd and the excitement of another day.

As for Benjamin Dulany, he spent his last years on Shuter's Hill overlooking the Nation's Capital. The view he enjoyed was preserved on canvas by John Gadsby Chapman, grandson of the Gadsby tavernkeeper. Dulany died in 1818 and was buried on his property on Shuter's Hill.

Walk north on South St. Asaph Street to Cameron Street. Turn right to:

GEORGE WASHINGTON'S TOWN HOUSE
508 Cameron Street

Private residence.

This small house is the only replica of an eighteenth century building closely associated with historic personages in Alexandria to be reconstructed on the original site.

Washington bought the lot, number 118, and completed the building on it in 1765. The house provided convenient and comfortable quarters for him when business or bad weather kept him in town, served as an office and, in modern terms, often as a guest house for his friends. On one occasion he made it available to young Dr. William Brown as living quarters. On another, he offered it rent free to his nephew, Bushrod Washington.

Replica of George Washington's small
town house.

At one point during the Revolutionary War when several British men-of-war lay just below the town, and George Mason, reporting that the British had already plundered several homes, was preparing to evacuate Gunston Hall, General Washington seriously considered enlarging this house and bringing his family here from the more vulnerable position of Mount Vernon. The danger passed and with it the plan. The little house remained as it was, serving a variety of purposes and continuing to belong to the Washington family after George Washington's death. Mrs. Washington left it to a nephew who subsequently sold it.

By the mid 1850s the old structure was in such dilapidated condition that it was torn down. Fortunately, a history-conscious neighbor who had lived across the street for a long time, Mary Jane Stewart, made an amateur but invaluable sketch of the house together with a description as she remembered it, "for posterity."

During the early 1940s a Washington architect, Deering Davis, with the assistance of the curatorial staff at Mount Washington, prepared a conjectural restoration drawing of the house. The site on which it had stood remained vacant, turned into a garden. In 1960, the late former governor of Guam, Richard Barrett Lowe, and his wife accepted the challenge to rebuild the house as nearly like the original as meticulous research made possible. It was a labor of love and pride. Bricks and stones from the excavation were used in the fireplace and as lintels for the windows set in the foundations. The mantel, woodwork and other details in the living room are copied from those used in one of the rooms which Washington is known to have planned in the home of his mother, Mary Ball Washington, in Fredericksburg, Virginia.

Today the little house has mellowed and acquired a nearly-authentic patina of age that makes it very charming.

Cross Cameron Street and walk west (toward Washington Street) to:

LORD FAIRFAX HOUSE
607 Cameron Street

Private residence.

The Lord Fairfax House is best viewed first from across Cameron Street in order to give visitors opportunity to study its interesting architecture, different from the familiar mid-Georgian houses built in the eighteenth century. This was erected early in the nineteenth century as a winter town house for Thomas, ninth Lord Fairfax and Baron of Cameron, who had extensive holdings south of Alexandria and spent much of his time there.

The house was built by William Yeatman, a New Hampshire merchant and ship owner who moved to Alexandria about 1800 and subsequently became an architect and building contractor. Note the curving steps and iron railings which extend over the sidewalk and the deeply-recessed double front doors under a well-proportioned brick arch. Above the arch, a narrower two-story white stucco arch contains the center hall windows of the second and third stories; and between the floors, a narrow course of white stone adds interesting detail that is reminiscent of fine old English houses. The first floor front windows have brick arches and shaped green shutters, while the smaller top floor windows rise nearly to the over-hang of the roof. A graceful spiral staircase—quite the grandest one in Alexandria—is lighted as it mounts upward by a skylight in the roof.

The Fairfax family had been closely associated with Northern Virginia from the time that young Thomas, sixth Lord Fairfax, inherited substantial property here and, subsequently, became the largest land-owner in the colony. Three members of the family, Thomas, his relative Colonel William Fairfax, who owned an estate, Belvoir Manor, south of Alexandria; and William's son, George William Fairfax, were among the first trustees of Alexandria. The latter two were also successful bidders for choice lots on the first day of auction.

The Fairfaxes were Tories, content to remain British colonials and to enjoy their vast Virginia land holdings. As the patriotic fervor preceding the Revolutionary War swept through Colonial America, the George William Fairfaxes left for England, where they had frequently made long visits, never to return; but other members of the family remained in Virginia. One was Bryan Fairfax, a half-brother of George William who was nearly contemporary with George Washington and maintained a lifetime friendship with him in spite of their political differences. Bryan, a devoutly religious man, spent most of his adult life at Mount Eagle, his estate south of Alexandria; but after becoming an ordained clergyman he served for a brief time as rector of Christ Church before succeeding to the title as eighth Lord Fairfax in 1800. The title then passed to his son, Thomas, who owned this house which, at his death, went to his son, Dr. Orlando Fairfax, a prominent and successful physician. By that time the title "Lord" had been dropped by American members of the family, many of whom continue their close association with Alexandria. The line and the title continue today in England.

In the 1860s loyalties were once again strained as war clouds gathered. After Alexandria was invaded by Union forces early in the Civil War, the Lord Fairfax House was confiscated under an Act of Congress permitting the seizure of property of Confederate loyalists. Fortunately for the owner, arrangements were quickly made by Governeur Morris of New York, a relative by marriage, to return this property.

Today this great old house with its beautiful garden partially hidden behind a high brick wall is only steps away from modern Alexandria's busiest thoroughfare; yet its heritage has endowed the house with the dignity and sense of privacy that belong to the remoteness of a country estate. From the windows of the long two-story ell that extends back into the garden, the view is of old trees, spreading shrubbery and, in season, of well tended flower beds.

Walk two doors west to:

GENERAL HENRY (Lighthorse Harry) LEE HOUSE
611 Cameron Street

Private residence · Home for a brief period of General Lee, father of Confederate General Robert E. Lee, and his family.

The inscription on the marker placed near the corner of this fine late eighteenth century brick house, counterpart architecturally to the house at 609, tells of its association with the great Revolutionary War hero and statesman. General Lee and his second wife, Anne Hill Carter, with their four children moved here from the Lee estate, Stratford, in Westmoreland County.

The family was scarcely settled and the children placed in school when war clouds gathered once more over the beloved country for which the dashing "Lighthorse Harry" had fought so bravely. England had not accepted gracefully the loss of her rich American colonies in 1783. After repeated harassment of American shipping on the high seas, President James Madison, on June 1, 1812, recommended to Congress that war be declared against Britain for blockading foreign and American ports and impressing American seamen into British service. The War of 1812 had begun.

General Lee who, by this time was also former Governor of Virginia, was fifty-five years old; however, when offered a commission from Congress as a major general, he was quick to accept. The General was full of vigor and, like the old war horse that he was, smelled the excitement of action.

Tragedy came quickly for him. Word arrived that he had become entangled with an angry mob in Baltimore and was severely wounded. The remaining six years of his life were racked by ill health and misfortune.

Before his death he moved his family into the more commodious residence at 607 Oronoco Street where they would be closer to relatives; and it was here that Mrs. Lee and her children lived until young Robert left for West Point and his own distinguished military career.

Walk to the corner of N. Washington Street, turn right and north on Washington Street to Lee Corners (intersection of Washington and Oronoco Streets) to:

THE HOUSES AT LEE CORNERS

LEE-FENDALL HOUSE
429 North Washington Street

Open as a house museum · Gift shop · Small admission charge.

Lee Corners is the unofficial name given to the intersection of North Washington and Oronoco streets. Three handsome eighteenth century houses that were home to many members of the Virginia Lees are located here within sight of each other.

Entrance hall of the Lee-Fendall House showing architectural detail.

Top left, Mary Lee Fitzhugh, who was married in the Fitzhugh-Lee house in 1804 to George Washington Parke Custis, grandson of Martha Washington. *Top right*, General Robert E. Lee who lived in the Fitzhugh-Lee house as a boy and married a grand-daughter of William Fitzhugh. *Bottom left*, William Fitzhugh of Chatham (1741–1809) moved into the Fitzhugh-Lee house in 1799. *Bottom right*, Mrs. William Henry Fitzhugh Jr. whose husband inherited the house at 607 Oronoco Street.

The first to be erected is the large white building on the southeast corner. It was recently purchased by the Virginia Trust for Historic Preservation and was opened to the public in 1974 as a house museum. The house contains a growing collection of furniture, furnishings and personal belongings of members of the distinguished Lee family.

The one-half acre lot on which the house was built in 1785 was owned briefly by General "Lighthorse Harry" Lee. He sold the lot to Philip Richard Fendall, a distant relative and second husband of his mother-in-law; and it was Fendall who built the handsome residence. In it throughout the years up to 1903 lived twenty-one members of the Lee-Fendall family. In more recent years the house was the home of the labor leader, John L. Lewis, and his family.

The house has undergone considerable remodeling during the 180 years of its history. The formal Federal style architecture of its present exterior, with the long fifteen-pane windows on the first floor and the interestingly-latticed small ones under the roof line would place the house in a later period except for its well documented history. Much of the fine interior woodwork is believed to be original.

Now designated as the Lee-Fendall House, the residence is being maintained in the atmosphere of its earlier years as a memorial to General "Lighthorse Harry" Lee. He was the oldest of the four sons of Colonel Henry Lee and Lucy Grymes Lee, all of whom are associated in some way with the Lee Corners houses. While General Lee never lived in this house he was often a visitor here in company with his close friend and former commander-in-chief, then President George Washington, during and after Lee's own service as governor of Virginia (1791–1794). It was he who, on December 26, 1799, paid tribute to Washington in words familiar to every American: "First in war, first in peace, and first in the hearts of his countrymen," and then the less familiar conclusion, "he was second to none in the humble and endearing scenes of private life."

Boyhood home of Robert E. Lee · Owned and maintained as a national shrine by Lee-Jackson Memorial, Inc. · Gift and souvenir shop · Open 9 a.m. to 5 p.m. daily · Small admission charge.

The house at 607 Oronoco Street, identified by its marker as the "Boyhood Home of Robert E. Lee," had been associated with historic personages and events in Alexandria for some years before the family of General Henry (Lighthorse Harry) Lee came to live in it. This is one of a pair of houses begun in 1793 by John Potts. It was completed in 1795 and sold in 1799 to Colonel William Fitzhugh, whose mansion, Chatham, on the Rappahannock River, near Fredericksburg, was one of the great houses of the period. While he was living on his estate at Chatham, which was developed between 1765 and 1775, Colonel Fitzhugh had served as a member of the Virginia House of Burgesses (1772–1775), the Revolutionary Conventions of 1775 and 1776, and of the Continental Congress. Colonial leaders and patriots knew well the hospitality he provided there. Of it, George Washington wrote: "I have put my legs oftener under your mahogany at Chatham than anywhere else in the world, and have enjoyed your good dinners, good wine and good company more than any other." When the Fitzhughs moved into this town house, Washington was often a guest here, too, as his diary shows. On April 3, 1799, he records, "In the evening went to Alex's and lodged myself at Mr. Fitzhugh's."

Then comes the entry of November 17, 1799:

"A very heavy and thick fog—Morning calm, & Mer. at 41. About 1 Oclock the Sun came out and the afternoon was pleasant.—Went to Church in Alexandria & dined with Mr. Fitzhugh."

The older daughter of Colonel and Mrs. Fitzhugh, Anne Randolph, was married to a son of Dr. James Craik, who lived

Washington often arrived as a guest
at this open door.

at 210 Duke Street. The other daughter, Mary Lee, was married in this house in 1804 to George Washington Parke Custis, grandson of Martha Washington. It was their only daughter, Mary, who was married to the young army officer, Robert Edward Lee.

General Henry (Lighthorse Harry) Lee brought his family to Alexandria in 1811 from the Lee family estate, Stratford, in Westmoreland County, one of the oldest and most monumental of the great brick mansions of Virginia. One reason for the move was the need to be near good schools for the growing family of young Lees. At the time, Charles Carter was 13; Anne, 11; Smith, 9; and Robert Edward, 4. The family lived first in a house at 611 Cameron Street, but moved into this larger residence in a neighborhood of relatives late in 1811.

The nearness of relatives was particularly comforting when Mrs. Lee learned the news of the death of her husband in 1818 at Cumberland Island, Georgia, on the estate of his old companion-in-arms, General Nathanael Greene, while en route home from Barbados, where he had gone in search of improved health. It was in this house, in the drawing room to the left of the entrance, that the widowed Mrs. Lee received the Marquis de Lafayette on his visit to Alexandria in October of 1824. Whether the 17-year-old Robert, who was already strong enough to lift his ailing mother in and out of the old family carriage for her daily outings, was invited to have tea with the French nobleman that afternoon, we do not know. However, he was listed as a member of the Civic Escort in connection with the various festivities connected with the official visit.

A bit of near doggerel by Benjamin Hallowell, the Quaker schoolmaster who lived in the companion house at 609 Oronoco Street where he was maintaining his excellent school at the time, throws more light on the enthusiasm over the Lafayette visit than many pages of chronicled activities. In high

Top, Mrs. Lee's bedchamber. *Bottom*, Lafayette Room where the widowed Mrs. Henry Lee served tea to the Marquis when he came to pay his respects in 1824.

Photos by Elsa S. Rosenthal, courtesy of Lee-Jackson Memorial, Inc.

mood, having been married at the height of the visit, Hallo-well wrote:

Each lover of liberty surely must get
Something in honor of Lafayette.
There's a Lafayette watch-chain, a Lafayette hat,
A Lafayette this and a Lafayette that;
But I wanted something as lasting as life—
And took to myself a Lafayette wife.

Young Robert E. Lee had received good schooling at the Alexandria Academy. By early 1825 he was studying mathe-matics with Hallowell, and in June of that year entered West Point. His mother soon left this old house to spend her few remaining years making her home with relatives. She died in 1829—the year of her son's graduation.

The house is furnished and maintained today in the manner and spirit of the years of occupancy by the Lee family. The brick-paved courtyard and surrounding garden provide a setting in which the present fades into the past and the men, women and little children who have called this old house "home" become very real to today's guests.

Cross North Washington Street to:

EDMUND JENNINGS LEE HOUSE
428 North Washington Street

Private residence.

This beautiful brick Georgian house was erected on a half-acre lot which Charles Lee, the second son of Colonel Henry Lee and his wife, Lucy Grymes Lee, bought in 1796. He sold the property in January, 1801, to his younger brother, Ed-mund Jennings who, with his family, had been living in a

A long gallery on the south side of the Edmund Jennings Lee House overlooks a pool and beautiful garden.

"handsome, convenient, three-story brick house . . . in King Street, a few doors west of Pitt Street," according to the FOR RENT advertisement he had placed in the local newspaper in December of that year. Lee and his family occupied the new house for many years.

It is a particularly well-built house, nearly square, three stories high, with a long two-story ell which has a delightful porch along the garden side. The old house is magnificently furnished and the property is meticulously maintained by the present owners.

In contrast to his dashing, colorful oldest brother, General "Lighthorse Harry," Edmund Jennings Lee was a studious lawyer and a devoted churchman. After the Revolutionary War when efforts were made by the State of Virginia to confiscate the glebe lands, set aside in colonial times for the use of the various parish churches, and to divide the proceeds from the sale of these lands "among the poor," Lee represented the vestry of Christ Church in the controversy. He brought such forceful and sensible arguments into the controversy that the decision of the State was declared unconstitutional. Christ Church was allowed to retain its glebe lands which were shortly sold for the benefit of the local parish.

Lee was elected mayor of Alexandria in 1814, and served for four years.

Walk south on North Washington Street to:

LLOYD HOUSE
220 North Washington Street

Open. Inquire at Bicentennial Center about hours.

The recently restored Lloyd House has stood proudly on North Washington Street since it was erected in 1793 by

Looking toward the garden gazebo, Edmund Jennings Lee House.

The beautifully pedimented doorway of the Lloyd House is one of the best in Alexandria.

James Hooe. Its exterior architecture is in the mid-Georgian style so popular in Alexandria in the late eighteenth century. The doorway is regarded as one of the finest among many similarly pedimented in Alexandria.

After the death of the builder, the commodious residence was used for about six years by the Quaker schoolmaster, Benjamin Hallowell, for his school which had then outgrown its quarters in his residence nearby on Oronoco Street. The house was sold to John Lloyd at public auction after the death of Mrs. Hooe. To it in 1832 he brought his lovely wife, Anne Harriotte Lee, daughter of Mr. and Mrs. Edmund Jennings Lee, who had grown up in the similar house of her parents at 428 North Washington Street.

Mrs. Lloyd was a first cousin of Robert E. Lee who, with his wife and children from Arlington House, were often guests of their Lloyd relatives. Present-day members of the family still tell their grandchildren about the Sunday in late May of 1861 when the handsome ruddy-faced General Lee, who had the day before resigned his commission in the United States Army, learned here that he had been named Commander of the Army of Northern Virginia by the Virginia State Legislature. Torn between love of country and devotion to his native Virginia, this gallant leader surely had long thoughts about the serious trouble ahead on which he had commented sometime earlier in the Apothecary Shop on South Fairfax Street.

The peace of that quiet Sunday afternoon, shattered by the outbreak of war, came back to North Washington Street in time, but the gracious hostess of that day did not survive to see it although her descendants rounded out nearly a century of family occupancy. Changes in ownership and the ravages of time took toll of the Lloyd House then, as was the case with a number of other historic residences of the same period; however, pride in the hearts of a new generation of residents of Alexandrians refused to let this house be demolished or dwarfed by overshadowing commercialism.

The house was purchased by the Alexandria Historical Restoration and Preservation Commission. Now handsomely and appropriately restored under the supervision of Walter C. Macomber, restoration architect for the White House and other historic buildings, it is being readied to serve as a repository for a large collection of Lee papers and other *Virginiana* in the possession of the Alexandria Library which, itself, has been an important part of the old town since the year in which the Lloyd House was built. In its new capacity, the Lloyd House will once more be the meeting place of the past and the present.

Houses with a Past
and a Presence

THROUGHOUT the old port section of Alexandria pride in ownership of private residences is apparent in gleaming brass knockers, freshly-painted woodwork, carefully planned gardens—the well-kept look that comes from caring about where and how one lives. There is no residential section as apart from a business district. Private residences and shops live together congenially, as they always have, often combined in the same building. There are spacious second floor drawing rooms, libraries lined to high ceilings with books, dining rooms in which a dozen or more guests can be comfortably seated as candlelight is reflected in polished silver—all within a few feet of busy streets.

Many of the old houses have carefully documented records going back through generations of owners to the eighteenth century. A few have been occupied by members of the same family since they were new. Some depend upon the evidence of worn old beams, stone foundations and fragments of in-

129

An air of elegance surrounds the house
at 711 Prince Street.

terior woodwork to vouch for their early origin. Others began as dependencies to large town houses—kitchens, service areas, carriage houses—and have been turned into comfortable homes. And every one of these houses has its own special presence, its own history.

Tours of Old Houses are regular features of life in Alexandria, as popular with local residents as with visitors. As many as one hundred old houses are open to visitors for brief periods every year, under the sponsorship of several organizations. The Alexandria Association for Restoration and Preservation has for many years held its annual Spring Events the first week-end in May. Garden Club Week in Virginia features old houses and gardens as a part of its spring program. A long-established fall tour is sponsored for the benefit of the Alexandria Hospital by its Auxiliary Board; and the Christmas Walk of the Alexandria Community Y features old houses elaborately decorated for the holidays as a part of a gala week of activities. There are other tours, too, particularly during the Bicentennial observance years extending to 1983. Information about these tours is regularly available at the Visitors Centers.

THE FLOUNDER HOUSES

The so-called flounder house is an architectural anomaly that may well be unique to Alexandria. In appearance, it is a half-house, as if a conventional colonial-style house had been cut down the ridge pole the long way of the roof, leaving a completely flat side, devoid of windows or doors. The opposite side which usually faces south, has a double balcony or a second-floor porch extending along its length, opening upon a garden.

No records have yet been discovered that tell who originated this type of architecture, who built the first flounder house, and why. But nearly everyone in Old Alexandria has a ready explanation. The flounder designation is easy enough to understand in a town on a river. The houses resemble the fish—flat with eyes on one side. There are three explanations which, taken together, are reasonably acceptable. One lies in the Act of Founding of the town. Purchasers of the first lots that were auctioned were required to erect buildings within two years or forfeit the lots. Confronted with a time limit and a scarcity of building materials and trained workmen—even funds—some lot holders might well have met minimum building requirements with a structure that could be considerably enlarged at a later time.

Another explanation for the flounder houses is the high cost of glass for windows. In colonial times, glass imported from England was costly partly because England, herself, was importing much of her own glass from other countries. During the years 1769–1770 there was much correspondence between the Virginia House of Burgesses and the British Parliament regarding removal of the unpopular glass tax. After the Revolutionary War, tariff barriers continued to exist, now between the new states. In 1785, at Gadsby's Tavern, then known as City Tavern, there was a meeting of the Maryland-Virginia Commission to settle a dispute regarding the excessive tariff duties imposed on goods, including glass, transported across the Potomac. Four years later, the governor of Virginia was negotiating to have glass for public buildings "imported from Philadelphia with no duty to be demanded."

A third explanation of flounder houses lies in old English law which did not guarantee to a builder the right to light and air. The one-half acre lots which were first sold in Alexandria soon began to be split into smaller lots, and with the requirement that buildings be erected on the street, the thought might well have occurred to some builders that there was a decided advantage to a house with one flat, windowless side, against which another house might be erected. Certainly, old English building regulations did not apply in Alexandria, but neither were property owners protected by the zoning regulations and building restrictions now in force.

FOUR INTERESTING FLOUNDER HOUSES

202 Duke Street

This lovely old house is "free-standing," built well back from the street, surrounded by a garden and a high brick wall. The best view of the high, flat, unwindowed side of the house is from the grassy alley entrance around the corner on South Lee Street.

321 South Lee Street

Here is a small flounder house on a narrow lot, with the entrance on the south garden side. The house at 319 has been built against the high, flat side of the flounder which extends several feet above its neighbor. The best view is from across the street.

317 South St. Asaph Street

Only a few feet back from the street behind its dark green picket fence, this flounder house has had some windows cut in the north side. The long balcony along the south side of the house hangs above a beautiful garden with a measure of privacy scarcely to be expected in so central a location.

Church office of the Old Presbyterian Meeting House
(In the rear of the church, entered from 321 South Fairfax Street or from 316 South Royal Street.)

Visitors may view this flounder house from all sides. It was built in 1787 by Robert Brockett to serve as a parsonage. In 1951, the house was completely renovated to be used for a pastor's study and church office. It is a three-story building, with the high blind side immediately adjacent to St. Mary's Catholic Church next door. Four small windows have been cut into the flat surface, and the line between the original con-

Flounder house, 321 South St. Asaph Street.

struction and a more recent addition is clearly traced in the brick.

From the 300 block of South Fairfax Street walk north to Prince Street and turn right. Captains Row is the 100 block.

CAPTAINS ROW
100 block of Prince Street

Private residences.

There are 28 doorways in this short block running westward from the waterfront which give access to a group of the most delightful and surprisingly spacious houses in old Alexandria. Although the buildings, of brick for the large part, stand shoulder to shoulder and flush with the sidewalk, they have rear windows that overlook quiet gardens. And they are full of interesting details and ever so many tales.

During the years when Alexandria was one of the principal ports of entry in the country—it still is such a port—some of the captains whose vessels docked at the wharves here made Alexandria home port, building their homes convenient to the river. This is why the block is called Captains Row. The block needs to be walked slowly to savor its special charm. Indeed, traffic never hurries along Captains Row. The cobblestones see to that. Who can say with documented accuracy that the stones are imported ballast, laid under duress by Hessian prisoners, those German mercenaries hired to suppress rebellious colonials during the American Revolution, or whether they came prosaically from the Potomac River? They may have been laid as a part of the general paving program of the town that, when better surfacing was available, provided foundation stones for a number of buildings and mountings for historic monuments. The important fact is that the cobble-

Captains Row, 100 block of Prince Street, showing cobblestones.
Courtesy the Alexandria Tourist Council.

stones are here, and residents of the Row would count their removal desecration.

Most of the houses, now all private residences, were originally used in part for business. The houses at 116 and 118, for instance, belonged to two Quaker sea captains, friends, who used the first floor of one building for showroom and merchandising and shared a common attic for storage. High on the east wall of a neighboring house is the old pulley by which bales and crates and sacks could be hauled to the third floor, above the family living quarters on the second floor. Young apprentices shared the attic rooms with the sacks which, often as not, provided them with beds. The sturdy old rafters whisper stories of miscreants with "proper connections" who could be—and were—passed stealthily from attic to attic, eluding pursuit and escaping through a variety of circuitous routes.

Each time one of these houses changes owners and undergoes renovation, new and interesting discoveries are apt to be made. A fragment of old sea wall was recently identified. Foundation timbers and stones are found behind a wall believed to be "original." Excavating in the cellars turns up all sorts of shards, perhaps a few foreign coins, buttons from a sea jacket.

Anytime is a good time to walk along Captains Row—early in the morning when there is mist over the river . . . on a wet afternoon when rain polishes the cobblestones . . . and after dark when the old-fashioned street lights cast shadows and an Old World atmosphere brings out the ghosts of the men who roamed the streets and waterfronts of the world but came home to find peace in these houses.

GENTRY ROW
200 block of Prince Street

Private residences.

Beginning at the Athenaeum on the corner of Prince and South Lee streets, in one block alone on Prince Street, are at least six eighteenth century town houses so architecturally distinguished that the term Gentry Row, recently coined, seems altogether appropriate. The houses are private residences, handsomely furnished, well maintained, and have been open often on tours as well as to architects and research students. They are certain to be open again.

207 Prince Street

The land on which this handsome buff-colored four-story brick house stands was acquired by William Fairfax, one of the original trustees of Alexandria, but was conveyed along

Gentry Row, 200 block of Prince Street, showing the George William Fairfax House in the foreground.

with other holdings in deeds recorded in 1753 and 1767 to his son, George William Fairfax. It was this young man, a contemporary (1730–1811) of George Washington, who was sent with him by Thomas, sixth Lord Fairfax, in March of 1748 on a surveying mission into the "wilderness country" near Winchester, where Greenway Court was built. George William and his father had both been present at the first auction of lots in Alexandria in 1749 and had purchased property.

George William Fairfax took an important part in the life of Alexandria, serving for a time as a member of the House of Burgesses. It was while he was in Williamsburg in that capacity that he met the lovely and lively Sally Carey who, at 17, became his bride. Fairfax had been educated in England where he had many friends, relatives, and some business interests. He and Sally were there on family business in 1757, but were back in Alexandria when he was commissioned as an officer in the Fairfax County Militia. The Fairfaxes returned to England for two years (1760–62). He had no sympathy with the rising tide of resentment in Virginia against British tyranny. As the crisis moved closer to war, he sold his property and in 1773 he and his wife returned to England to remain permanently. In spite of differing loyalties, they maintained friendly relations with the family at Mount Vernon and old friends in Alexandria.

The new owner was Robert Adam, a Scotsman of wealth, who succeeded William Fairfax as a trustee of Alexandria, and was first Master of the Masonic Lodge. The house was owned briefly by Captain John Harper, who built a number of the houses on Captains Row. It was then purchased by William Hodgson who conducted a dry goods business on the first floor, using the upper floors for family quarters.

The house has undergone numerous alterations since it was originally constructed, the most recent by its present owner. It is regarded as one of the finest of the eighteenth century houses in Alexandria and is furnished beautifully with the antiques that enhance its charm.

209 and 211 Prince Street

These two excellent eighteenth century town houses are often confused because the marker on 209 properly belongs to 211. The latter, as deeds show beyond doubt, was the house of Dr. Elisha Cullen Dick during the major part of his residence in Alexandria. Both Dr. Dick and Dr. James Craik lived in several houses before settling permanently in their own homes. For a time Dr. Craik lived in 209 Prince Street and Dr. Dick lived at 517 Prince Street.

Dr. Dick completed the study of medicine just at the close of the Revolutionary War. He was therefore a generation younger than Dr. Craik, who called him into consultation with Dr. Gustavus Brown during the last day of George Washington's final illness. He opposed the heavy bleeding of the patient, a practice in wide use at the time.

Mrs. Dick was a Quaker lady who, according to old accounts, persuaded her Episcopal husband to join her in the Society of Friends. Thereupon, he took his prized dueling pistols down to the bank of the Potomac River and threw them into the water. A watching fisherman must have recognized the value of the pistols for he rescued at least one of them and sold it. Dr. Dick discovered it in a shop window, reclaimed it; and in substantiation of this story you may see the dueling pistol which is on display in a cabinet in the hallway just outside the replica Masonic Lodge Room in the Memorial Building. It was presented by descendants of Dr. Dick, of whom there are many.

He is described as a highly versatile man, accomplished in science, music, literature, painting and horsemanship. As a doctor, he was particularly interested in public health problems and served as public health officer. He recognized two major causes of the plagues of yellow fever, cholera and smallpox: one was the contamination of drinking water by seepage from adjacent privy wells. The other was the spread of contagious diseases from affected persons arriving on the numerous vessels coming into Alexandria from foreign ports. His early insistence upon health regulations undoubtedly aided in the control of these diseases.

As an active member of the Alexandria-Washington Masonic Lodge 22, he officiated at the laying of the cornerstone of the District of Columbia at Jones Point in 1791, and served as mayor of the town in 1804.

213 and 215 Prince Street

The unpretentious entrances directly from the sidewalk into these two early houses give scant intimation of the interior spaciousness and elegance that make them architecturally important. The first floor is strictly utilitarian, for these were the houses of merchants who combined their show rooms and offices with residences. The house at 213 was owned by a William Hickman until 1800. Behind the 24-paned windows, a winding stairway leads to a second-floor drawing room with a wedge fireplace between two beautifully fluted pilasters with an over mantel and cornice. Comfortable, airy bedrooms on the third floor overlook gardens to the rear and rise so high above Prince Street in the front that one is scarcely aware of being in the center of town.

210 Prince Street

Augustine Washington was the first owner of the lot on which this house was built. It is known as the Swope House because Colonel Michael Swope, who come to Alexandria from Pennsylvania in the early 1780s, bought the property and greatly improved it. Here, as in other old houses in the area, there is reason to believe that the present building includes portions of an earlier structure. The excellent taste of Mrs. Swope is exemplified in the interior woodwork which ranks with the finest of the Georgian period. The furniture and furnishings of the house today are completely consistent with the taste of its first owner.

Eighteenth century furniture compliments the fine architecture of the house at 210 Prince Street.
Courtesy of Mrs. Hugh B. Cox.

NORTH OF KING STREET

The large building on the northeast corner of Cameron and North Fairfax Street was once a popular tavern. It was begun by John Dalton, one of the first trustees, who lived in the house just north of the tavern on Royal Street. This tavern, which has most recently served as the Anne Lee Memorial Home, was owned at one time by John Wise who also owned Gadsby's Tavern. It was called the Bunch of Grapes until it changed hands. Then, John Wise moved the sign across the street and gave the interesting name to what is now Gadsby's Tavern. The builder, John Dalton, was the great-grandfather of Ann Pamela Cunningham through whose dedicated efforts Mount Vernon was saved to become a national shrine.

The structure now serves a number of commercial purposes, including several antique shops, and is open to visitors. Through the garden gate at the rear of the building on Cameron Street where there are several small apartments you can glimpse delightful walled gardens. In the center of this block, against an old brick wall, is a marker indicating the location of the first lot that was auctioned.

Such pre-Revolution buildings as Carlyle House, Gadsby's Tavern, Christ Church and a number of private residences are easily located and identified by signs and historic markers. Others, erected under the early requirements that unless buildings within minimum requirements were put up within two years, owners of the lots must forfeit them, are not easily identified. You will find them as flounder wings behind or beside larger structures built after the Revolutionary War when building was resumed. Sometimes they are attached by hyphen-construction to a late eighteenth century or early nineteenth century building. Wherever you walk in Old Alex-

Twin arches at the
entrance of the
Married Houses, 211
North Fairfax St.

andria, watch for the angles of roof lines that show where
buildings have been joined. Watch for cobblestone alleys and
openings into gardens where you can trace in the pattern of
brick walls and the change from brick to clapboard over brick
the merging of a very old building into a newer one.

Every alley in Old Alexandria is worth investigating. Several of these are clearly marked by street signs such as Ramsay
Alley and Swift Alley, both extending through the blocks
from Fairfax Street to Lee Street. In these alleys you will discover private residences, gardens, craft shops, flounder wings
and dependencies of large on-street buildings. Even in the
busiest part of the city, just south of the Post Office on South
Washington Street, Number 10 Norton Alley is a delightful
private residence.

Back on North Fairfax Street, the eighteenth century house
at 211 is really two houses, often referred to as the Married
Houses. If you can close your eyes to the peeling paint on the
handsome arched doorways, the sagging shutters and an air of
general neglect, you may be able to visualize this great mansion as it once was and as it may become again. Some of Alexandria's finest old houses as they are today were once just as
close to being lost. The struggle against the crumbling of
aging walls and the decay of termite- and time-ridden timbers

The loggia is an architectural gem.

is a heavy responsibility to a town that is determined to preserve the past in its present.

This two-part house was built on land bought by John Dalton at the first auction in one of the oldest blocks to be developed. The house was bought from his daughter Catherine and her husband by Jonah Thompson, a wealthy merchant, by whose name the house continues to be known. The union of the two elements forming the mansion is apparent from the street in the mellow pink brick walls and the matching doorways, one of which has been turned into a window. The newer bricks encase a frame house believed to have resembled the Ramsay House.

If you walk down an alley along the north side of the house, you will find a wooden gate in the brick wall. Inside there is a garden of sorts—and more. The formal austerity of the house from the street side breaks into a graceful five-arched loggia in the Venetian manner, each arch supported by a superbly crafted slender classical column. Beneath the loggia are two large ground floor arched entrances into the thick-walled kitchen and service quarters of long-gone years.

Once the loggia and the ballroom above it looked out upon a garden that stretched to the river's edge, for the house was built above a curve of the river long ago filled in to provide ground for commercial purposes.

In the 200 block of North Royal Street, which is parallel to North Fairfax, away from the river, nearly every house bears a plaque identifying it as an historic building. The lovely brick house at 219, with its companion next door, is a good example of pre-Revolutionary War construction. Attention is called to the brickwork over the front door and windows and to the sandstone steps from the old Aquia Creek quarry. The house has a long flounder ell, a walled garden, and a brick coach-house.

The 300, 400 and 500 blocks of Queen Street have a variety of different houses: 312 Queen Street is a two-story house which was sold in 1752 by George William Fairfax and William Ramsay to "Daniel McCarty, Gent." George Washington, then 20 years of age, witnessed the signing of the deed which has been preserved. The house was owned from 1934 to 1946 by Admiral Halsey. By sharp contrast in the 500 block are some of the smallest, simplest houses one could imagine. At 523 Queen Street is a seven-foot wide residence, constructed in the alley space that once separated the houses on either side. How much room is in it? A living room and kitchen on the first floor, bedroom and bath upstairs. The houses at 514 and 516 are not much larger, but have a delightful formality about them, too. 511 is a flounder-type house.

Walking from Queen Street south on South St. Asaph Street you will come quickly to the intersection of Cameron and Prince streets. The large red brick building at 602 Cameron Street, now the home of the Alexandria Community Y, was the home of the novelist Frances Parkinson Keyes who, during the time that she owned it, restored and furnished the house in the manner of its architectural and historical period.

To the left from the intersection, at 517 Prince Street is a white clapboard house that is believed to be one of the oldest residences in Alexandria, dating to the 1750s, although it was at that time outside the original 1749 boundaries. It has the longest record of continued occupancy by the same family of any other house in the community, well over 150 years. This small on-street house has become a microcosm of life in Old Alexandria for although it has undergone innumerable changes, each prompted by the requirements of comfortable living, the old remains, too, and the family knows what was done, when and why. To the rear of the house behind a high brick wall are many reminders of earlier ways of life: the wash house with its old wooden tubs and bench close to the well, a small screen-enclosed summer room, a necessary house and other backyard facilities. Long ago the entrance was changed from the front of the building to a side porch, a later addition.

The house and the town have grown up together, from unpaved streets, wells, candles and oil lamps, fireplaces and horse drawn vehicles, within a framework of progress.

SOUTH OF KING STREET

First, in the 200 block of King Street are located the Chequire House at 202 and Gilpin House at 206–8. Both have shops on the first floor, as was the case with many of the houses in this area, and remarkably handsome living quarters on the upper floors. They were completed at approximately the same time, Chequire House in 1797 by a Frenchman whose

Smallest house in Old Alexandria is 7 feet wide,
was built in an alley at 523 Queen Street.

background was always somewhat of a mystery. He may have been a nobleman fleeing from the French Revolution. Certainly the interior woodwork of the living area of the house indicates an appreciation of good taste and elegance. Gilpin House was built in 1798 by Colonel George Gilpin who took a prominent part in social and community affairs until his death in 1813.

The 100 block of South Lee Street provides another surprise. It begins at a busy commercial intersection but within only a few feet becomes a quiet place of handsome houses and deep gardens. On the east side are houses that appear to be small, built by Captain John Harper, a sea captain, for his numerous daughters, but are larger and more comfortable than you might guess. Standing on the sidewalk in front of one such house, 120 South Lee Street, would you suspect that the sidewalk, itself, is the actual roof of an under-sidewalk cellar where, long ago, wine was stored? Or that the ground floor, below street level, opens onto a delightful hidden garden?

Walking down the east side of the 200 block of South Lee Street, one can see a marker on the house of George Johnston, at 224, which tells of his vital service to community and country in the period preceding the Revolutionary War. He was a brilliant lawyer, a member of the Virginia House of Burgesses and an early trustee of Alexandria. He made arrangements in 1757 to "have built a brick house . . . a livery and smoke house" on a lot he had purchased from Henry Fitzhugh, who acquired it at the first auction in 1749. He also owned a country place, Belle Vale, on what has become Telegraph Road, and had a law office at Prince and Lee Streets.

In the 300 and 400 blocks of South Lee Street, houses stand wall to wall, differing interestingly in materials, colors and styles of architecture, each reflecting the tastes of the owners and each worth more than a second glance. In the 500 block the east side of the street becomes a park, opening the vista of the Potomac River to the houses facing it.

Wilkes Street leads westward to South St. Asaph—the

street with the unusual name—that of a Bishop who cour-
ageously espoused the cause of liberty in England before the
Revolution. Here, walking northward, one sees for the most
part larger houses removed somewhat by time and distance
from the first development near the waterfront. The houses
are mostly Federal and Victorian in style, with imposing doorways, shining brass fittings and heavy knockers. Several of
these houses, notably those at 211 and in the next block at 307
South St. Asaph Street, are as distinctively furnished throughout as their exteriors suggest. Much of the cultural life of the
community centers around a knowledgeable appreciation of
proper restoration and preservation: exterior and interior architecture, furniture and rugs, paintings, porcelain and silver,
garden planning and planting. The Alexandria Forum, for
example, brings together every autumn 200 persons from all
parts of the country who during three days of lectures and
field trips study these subjects.

Walking westward on Prince Street across the busy intersection of South Washington Street, you may again be surprised to find great old houses so near the business area, and
yet in dignity and manner so remote from their commercial
surroundings that their privacy remains inviolate.

Such a house is 711 Prince Street. It began with a flounder
house set well back from the street, later to become the ell
of the larger house which was constructed by William Fowle,
a partner with Thomas Lawrason in the shipping business. He
was also active in organizing the Alexandria Water Company
and in the installing of a gas lighting system.

Five generations of the Fowle family lived in this house,
altering it, embellishing it, selling off part of the considerably
larger garden area, as circumstances and requirements dictated.

Today, the house wears an air of elegance. The entrance is
imposing with a shallow balcony supported by four slender
columns. In its spacious rooms life goes on in a manner consistent with the atmosphere of the house.

Old Churches and Cemeteries

W HEREVER English people settled in the new world, they brought with them the Church of England. The church and its ministers were supported throughout the colonial period by public taxation, payable in Virginia in tobacco, and its buildings were erected and maintained at public expense. Together with local civil authorities, the vestrymen of the parish churches were held responsible for "the maintenance of religion and all things pertaining thereto in the domain of charity and morals." A glebe, or plot of land, was customarily set apart for the benefit of the church; and in some areas and periods, the Church of England was the only one officially tolerated by civil authorities.

Truro Parish, in which Mount Vernon was located, was formed in 1732. Augustine Washington, father of George, was a member of the vestry, and his son was a vestryman from 1762 to 1784.

Lovely old Pohick Church, the parish church of Mount Vernon which was completed in 1772, is well worth visiting.

151

Christ Episcopal Church, where Washington and Lee worshiped.

Aquia Church, in Stafford County, is another such delightful old parish church, erected in 1752, and rebuilt after a fire in 1757, retaining the old walls.

CHRIST EPISCOPAL CHURCH
Columbus and Cameron Streets

Entrance to the church on Columbus Street, graveyard extending to North Washington Street, church offices and parish house at 118 North Washington Street · Open to visitors daily · Regular schedule of services.

Christ Church is a living landmark in Alexandria, in continuous full-time service as a church since it was completed in 1773. It was often referred to as "The Church in the Woods," before the town of Alexandria had yet stretched westward across Washington Street.

Was there an earlier chapel known as the Chapel of Ease on the spot where the church now stands, as one old manuscript says, or on Pitt Street near Princess, according to a well-worn legend? Reason bulwarks the existence of some place of worship, for the English settlers were accustomed to the offices of the Anglican Church. In the years between the building of Carlyle House in 1752 and the completion of Christ Church in 1772–73, a twenty year span, Alexandria was rapidly becoming a town. There were merchants and artisans, doctors and lawyers, shopkeepers and innkeepers, ships' captains and crews. There were births and deaths; and the offices of the church were needed locally and, in a normal manner, most surely were met.

Fairfax Parish, which included Alexandria and Mount Vernon, was established in 1765 when Truro Parish was divided. Washington had been a vestryman for Truro Parish since 1762. He was quickly elected to serve as vestryman in the new

Interior of Christ Church.
Courtesy the Alexandria Tourist Council.

parish and in that capacity had a part in the planning of the church. Indeed, well before it was completed he had selected his family pew, number 15, and was the first in the parish to pay for his selection. After the death of Martha Washington, her grandson, George Washington Parke Custis, presented to Christ Church the Washington family bible which had long been used at Mount Vernon.

The acre of land on which the church stands was a gift from John Alexander, a resident of Stafford County and a descendant of the original John, often referred to as the "Stirps of the American Line" [the founder]. In 1774 the church wardens exchanged with him the traditional penny for the gift.

Visitors to Christ Church today—and there are many thousands every year—are aware that this is no ordinary church building. In an Architectural Monograph on Alexandria edited by Russell F. Whitehead, the author, Henry Hodgman Saylor, states: "No student of early architecture of America thinks of Alexandria, Virginia, apart from these three great land-marks: Christ Church, the Carlyle House and Gadsby's Tavern; they *are* Alexandria."

Every line of the structure bespeaks the skilled planning of a master architect and builder. James Wren, believed to have been a descendant of the great Sir Christopher Wren, is given credit for designing the church. There is no doubt about his lettering the two tablets on either side of the altar. They contain the Lord's Prayer, the Apostles Creed and the Golden Rule. Written in black lettering on wood, the tablets have never been retouched. For this work the artist was paid eight pounds.

At the outset of the project, a man named James Parsons was employed to build the church. The records do not show why he was unable to complete the contract; however, after considerable irksome delay, John Carlyle who, among his other activities was in the construction business, agreed to complete the building. This he did, and it was duly accepted by the vestry on February 27, 1773. The Reverend Townsend Dade was the first rector.

The interior of the church is not large and seems to be, at first glance, almost simple in style; yet there is a nearly majestic dignity and grace in every line of the building, outside and inside. Architecturally, the six-sided high pulpit, centered before a Palladian window under a canopy suspended from the ceiling, belongs to the Ionic order. It rests upon a slender central support, and is mounted by a short flight of steps. The pews, which were originally square and high-backed, have been divided, with the exception of number 15, marked by a silver plate, the one so often occupied by members of the Washington family. Customarily now, on the Sunday nearest Washington's birthday, the President of the United States and his family worship in Christ Church, occupying the Washington pew.

The church lacked an organ, balconies, steeple and tower when it was completed in 1773; however, after the war, in

Bishop William
Meade, third
bishop of the
Episcopal Church
in Virginia, served
Christ Church
for a time.
Courtesy the Alexandria
Tourist Council.

1793, a second-hand organ, made in England, was presented as a gift. It served well at Christ Church, then was passed along to several other Virginia churches before it found a permanent home in the Smithsonian Institution. You may be fortunate enough to hear one of the frequent concerts presented on another organ, built especially to meet the continuing needs of the old church and recently installed.

As funds became available, balconies, steeple and tower were added. In each instance, the work was so carefully executed that the additions appear to be an integral part of the building from the beginning. Another addition, in 1817, was the cut-glass chandelier which was purchased in England by order of the vestry. It was first hung in the center of the ceiling and lit by tallow candles. Later, the chandelier was moved to its present location under the rear balcony. It is often used during special services in the church.

The Christ Church compound, including the historic sanctuary itself, parish houses facing North Columbus and North Washington streets, and the graveyard, is an island of serenity around which constantly flows the life of the city. As you stroll along brick walks under ancient trees among worn gravestones you are apt to reconstruct for yourself earlier scenes and events. Here George Washington stood in company with saddened townspeople as William Ramsay was laid to rest. You will find his grave. And here in a single ivy-covered mound lie 34 Confederate soldiers who died in prison camp.

On Sunday mornings members of the parish continue to worship, a part of the unbroken continuity that unites past and present in service and services.

OLD PRESBYTERIAN MEETING HOUSE
321 South Fairfax Street

Open to visitors (Inquire at Church Office) · Regular Sunday services.

The Presbyterians, too, have been in Virginia from the beginning. It was in 1611 that the Rev. Alexander Whitaker arrived at Jamestown to establish the first Presbyterian congregation in Virginia. He converted and in 1613 baptized Pocahontas, whom he also helped to educate.

Colonial America was substantially enriched by the migration of a quarter million Scotch-Irish followers of John Knox who, driven by religious fervor and economic necessity, arrived on these shores as permanent settlers between 1717 and 1775. Among those who came were some of the early leaders of Alexandria—Scottish merchants and their families. With

The Meeting House today.
Courtesy the Alexandria Tourist Council.

them came the influence of the Presbyterian Church although plans to erect a meeting house were not undertaken until 1772.

At that time, a group of interested families decided to call a Presbyterian minister to Alexandria although a chapel had not yet been constructed. When Richard Arell, a substantial businessman in the town, and his wife, Eleanor, offered to give a suitable lot for a church, the collection of funds was begun immediately. John Carlyle, who had done most of the construction of Christ Church, undertook to do the work. Before the outbreak of the Revolutionary War, a brick structure 60 x 50 feet was under cover.

It was often referred to as the Dissenting Church, as the Church of England was the only one officially recognized and

Sketch by Mary Jane Stewart of Old Presbyterian Meeting
House as it looked before a fire in 1835.
Courtesy the Virginia State Library.

tax supported. It was in this capacity that the Presbyterian
group offered its facilities to the Methodists and other groups
having no churches of their own. Religious intolerance was
not popular in this town where Anglicans, Presbyterians,
Methodists, Huguenots, Quakers and members of other religious societies daily did business with each other in a completely amicable atmosphere. It is left for a 24-year-old soldier
of fortune named Nicholas Cresswell who arrived in Alexandria from Liverpool in the winter of 1774 to provide in his
journal an "outsider's view" of church life in the community.
Under date of November 6, he wrote: "Went to a Presbyterian meeting. They are a lot of rebellious scoundrels,
nothing but political discourse instead of religious lectures."

The completion of the building was delayed until after the
Revolution when a steeple and galleries were added. The out-

standing pastor of this period was Dr. James Muir, a native of Scotland, who served from 1789 to 1820. A handwritten report entitled "History of the Presbyterian Church at Alexandria, from its commencement in 1772 to the present date A. D. 1794," which is preserved in the files of the Presbyterian Historical Society, in Philadelphia, makes interesting reading in so far as the day-to-day life of the congregation reveals much about the times generally in Alexandria.

When news reached Alexandria via Dr. James Craik of the death of George Washington, Dr. Muir quickly gave instructions to toll the bell in the steeple, the only church bell in Alexandria at the time. It tolled until the burial at Mount Vernon took place four days later. As the road leading to Christ Church was considered to be nearly impassable because of winter weather, arrangements were made with Dr. Muir to have a memorial service for Washington in the Presbyterian Church. The newspaper, then the Alexandria *Times,* gave the information to the community thus: "The walking being bad to the Episcopal Church, the funeral sermon of George Washington will be preached at the Presbyterian Meeting House tomorrow at 11:30 o'clock."

Dr. Muir was so highly regarded that, at his death, he was buried in the church, near the pulpit, dressed in his gown and bands. A memorial tablet now indicates the place.

The meeting house had been in use for sixty-three years when, on July 6, 1835, during a severe summer thunder storm the spire of the steeple attracted lightning which quickly set ablaze the four-sided pyramidal roof. Within two hours, the building was severely damaged. "Everything totally consumed . . . nothing left but the walls . . . a shapeless mass of smoldering ruins." The bell had fallen from the steeple and was damaged beyond retrieve. The organ was gone, too.

There was some discussion about whether to rebuild on the old site or to seek a new location. Perhaps attachment to the graveyard behind the church where sleep so many of Alexandria's early leaders and their families influenced the decision to rebuild on the old foundations, in more than the purely physical sense. By November, 1836, plans were well under way and by July, 1837, two years after the fire, the church, still within the original dimensions, was completed and ready for service. A bell tower was erected in 1843, and in 1853 the building was enlarged by the addition of a vestibule, with stairs on either side leading to the balconies.

During the Civil War when Alexandria was occupied by Union forces the services of the church were restricted; and the meeting house and many of the larger buildings in the community were commandeered for hospital purposes.

The interior of the church today, following renovation in 1926, has a colonial simplicity and dignity that seem to take you back to the early days of Alexandria.

The graveyard behind the house is a quiet place, too, guarded by interesting rooflines, angles and neighboring buildings. Here is located the grave of an unknown soldier of the American Revolution, although he was not one of the more than 8,000 battle casualties. When workmen were excavating a foundation wall of the adjacent Catholic chapel they accidentally unearthed a coffin near the property line. In it were the remains of a man and a Revolutionary War uniform. A long search for old burial records provided scant information, simply: "January 19, 1821, an Old Revolutionary Soldier from Kentucky." The coffin was reinterred in an unmarked spot and nearly forgot through many years while spring rains fell, weeds tangled, and winter brought a white blanket of snow. Then, through the efforts of Mary Gregory Powell, author of the authoritative *History of Alexandria* (1928), attention was directed to the presence of the old grave. As a small girl, this daughter of the congregation had heard the story from her father and remembered the spot he had shown her. The imagination and interest of the National Society of the Children of the Revolution was captured; and as a result these young Americans, mindful of their heritage, requested permission to place a suitable marker on the grave and to make it their special historic shrine. On Memorial Day every year representatives of the group bring their floral offering to place on the grave over which the Mount Vernon Guard stands vigil from dawn to dusk. The grave is surrounded by older graves whose worn stones read like a Who's Who of early Alexandria. Here lie John Carlyle and Dr. James Craik, Colonel Dennis Ramsay, Richard and Eleanor Arell, and William Hunter, Jr., born in Scotland in 1731, and founder of the St. Andrew's Society of Alexandria. Each September the present-day members of this ancient band of Scotsmen come with their bagpipes to salute their founder, and the sad, nostalgic strains of old Scotch tunes fill the air.

ST. MARY'S CATHOLIC CHURCH AND CEMETERY
300 block of South Royal Street (Church)
900 block of South Washington Street (Cemetery)

Open to visitors · Regular masses.

"Keep up religion of the Church of England, as near as may be. Avoid all fractions and needless novelties which only tend to the disturbance of peace and unity . . ."

This was the instruction issued in 1621 by the Virginia Company to Church of England ministers in Colonial Virginia. It was formulated into law in 1642 in the Virginia Act of Uniformity.

In the early seventeenth century England, herself, was adjusting to the clash between Catholics and Protestants that had rent the country, partly as a result of the marital problems of Henry VIII, and had caused royal heads to roll. It had resulted, in 1534, in the Act of Supremacy; and in 1603 had brought James I to the throne.

The right of an individual to worship in freedom was a new concept growing in the minds of religious leaders, but awaiting legal implementation. This came in the oldest of the English colonies in America in 1776 when the Virginia State Convention adopted George Mason's Bill of Rights. Following that, in 1785, came "The Act Establishing Religious Freedom."

Here in Alexandria there were some Catholics among the earliest residents. Where they worshiped and how are questions answered in part only by legend—a little log cabin in the woods. Well-documented, however, are the good offices of Colonel John Fitzgerald, at one time a young aide to General Washington, and subsequently mayor of Alexandria. Just as General Daniel Roberdeau, a French Huguenot who came to Alexandria shortly after the Revolution, opened his imposing house at 418 South Lee Street for early meetings of the Methodists in the community, so Colonel Fitzgerald extended the hospitality of his house at 106 South Lee Street to his fellow Catholics.

The first Catholic church was built in 1795. It was a brick building, never fully completed, located some distance south of the town on property that is now a part of the old Catholic cemetery on South Washington Street at Church Street. It served the small parish for about fifteen years until church leaders purchased from the Methodists a small meeting house and a smaller parsonage in what was then known as Chapel Alley, in the 300 block of Duke Street. The property cost $900. A bell tower was built and the buildings enlarged.

The sanctuary and major portion of the present imposing stone church were erected in 1826.

Visitors who step into the small church-side garden will be rewarded with an interesting view of surrounding roof lines and angles showing how buildings have grown through the years.

ALEXANDRIA NATIONAL CEMETERY
Wilkes Street

Open daily 8 a.m. to 5 p.m. · Memorial Day 8 a.m. to 7 p.m.

There is a place of deep peace and eternal quiet so close to the business center of modern Alexandria that thousands of persons pass nearby every day without suspecting its existence.

This is the Alexandria National Cemetery. It is located at the western terminus of Wilkes Street, entered through tall iron gates and protected by a wall. Here from the top of a tall flagpole the Stars and Stripes catch the breeze from dawn to dusk above the graves of veterans of three wars. No poppies grow as in the battlefield graveyards of France; but the grass is always green and neatly clipped, the evergreens and brightly-berried shrubs well-tended, and the white marble markers—so very many of them—stand at attention.

The Cemetery dates to Civil War times, before Arlington National Cemetery was opened. Alexandria was occupied by Union forces at the outset of the four-year struggle. Here a large hospital and convalescent center was maintained, with many of the large buildings of the town requisitioned for hospital purposes. It was a sad time for the town. Everyday life was very much restricted, even to the curtailment of most church services. The notes of taps sounding again and again from the cemetery were a painful reminder to the town's citizens, most of whom had followed General Lee in loyalty.

During World Wars I and II the National Cemetery continued to be used. Today, with only a few vacant spaces, it is a hallowed spot for those who still make pilgrimages there, especially on Memorial Day when the graves are bright with wreaths and flowers and the gates stay open two hours later than usual.

3 Enshrined Treasures

Bronze monument of Confederate soldier faces
south after Appomattox.

GEORGE WASHINGTON MASONIC
NATIONAL MEMORIAL
King Street and Russell Road

Open daily 9 a.m. to 5 p.m. · No admission charge · Tour guides on duty.

Visitors to the summit of the Masonic Memorial which rises 333 feet above the highest point of land in Alexandria are rewarded on a clear day with a magnificent panorama that extends for twenty miles in every direction.

A heavy bronze door gives access to a well-railed parapet which encircles the lofty tower. From the parapet you can look straight down King Street to the Potomac River where old Alexandria nestles along the bank and beyond to the Maryland shore fading in the distance. Looking southward, you can follow the river for miles, identifying the thick grove of trees that surrounds Mount Vernon. Westward beyond the spires of new churches and the Virginia Theological Seminary is the Alexandria home of Gerald Ford, 38th President of the United States. Northward is spread the whole panorama of the city of Washington, the Capitol, Washington Monument, National Cathedral and other recognizable landmarks.

167

Pastel portrait of George Washington by William Williams.

When the Founding Fathers decided to move the capital of the new United States from New York City where, on April 30, 1789, Washington had been inaugurated, to a more central location, the present Washington area was selected. In 1793, James Madison, then a member of the House of Representatives, was named chairman of a congressional committee to decide upon the site for the capitol. With enthusiastic approval of Thomas Jefferson, then Secretary of State, whose love of magnificent vistas had already determined the hill-crest location of his beloved Monticello, Madison recommended Shuter's Hill, which at the time was well outside the town of Alexandria.

President Washington did not accept the recommendation: one discovers that much of the property on or around this hilltop was owned by members of the Washington family. The conflict of interest issue is not new to this generation. Old Alexandria may owe the preservation of its eighteenth century buildings, however, to this decision by Washington. In August of 1814 when British vessels sailed up the Potomac River, General Ross captured the new city of Washington, set fire to the Capitol, the White House and the Navy Yard.

When the present site had been approved and construction started, President Washington, on September 18, 1793, laid the southeast cornerstone of the north section of the Capitol with Masonic ceremonies, using a small silver trowel which was fashioned by the Alexandria silversmith, John Duffey, and which is among the priceless treasures preserved here.

The hilltop that President Washington rejected served many purposes through the years. Fading old pictures from the 1860s show the barracks erected here by Union forces; and in 1907 when Alexandria celebrated its Tercentennial, Shuter's Hill was a popular golf course. In 1908, the historic property was purchased for $25,000 to serve as a park to the memory of Washington. On the 120th anniversary of his first inauguration as President of the United States, the park was dedicated in the presence of President William Howard Taft.

The cornerstone of the park was laid by Washington's old lodge, now known as the Alexandria-Washington Lodge. Meantime, sentiment throughout the country was growing among members of the Masonic Fraternity to erect a memorial to Washington that would safeguard the relics and treasures in possession of the Alexandria Lodge of which he was the first Master. The cornerstone of this building was laid November 1, 1923, using the same small silver trowel with which Washington had laid the cornerstone of the Capitol. The Alexandria Masons had the assistance on this occasion of President Calvin Coolidge and Chief Justice Taft. When the building was dedicated in 1932, President Herbert Hoover assisted in the dedicatory rites.

Today, safely enshrined within the marble walls of the Memorial in one comparatively small hall on the second floor, is the largest collection of authentic articles intimately associated with George Washington and his eighteenth century Alexandria friends and associates yet to be assembled in the city. Other treasures are in the Memorial Museum.

The hall is a replica of the Alexandria-Washington Lodge Room. The original Lodge Room was built over the Courthouse, on Cameron, Fairfax and Royal streets.

On May 19, 1871, the entire building including the lodge quarters was destroyed by fire. Most of the furniture, all the records, the Williams portrait of Washington, the Master's Chair from Mount Vernon, and many of the most valuable relics were saved by exceptional heroism of lodge members. Alas, in spite of their best efforts, lost for all time were the bier upon which the corpse of Washington was borne to the tomb at Mount Vernon, Washington's military saddle and card tables, many of his original letters in frames, a bust of John Paul Jones which had been presented to Washington by Lafayette and which had long adorned the dining room at Mount Vernon, together with the flag from Jones' *Bon Homme Richard*. Also lost was the flag of the Independent Blues of Alexandria, used in the War of 1812 when British

warships pointed their guns upward from the foot of King Street, and a particularly prized portrait of Lafayette.

When a new City Hall and Market House were planned, arrangements were made for the construction of a new Masonic Hall, too, to occupy practically the same location in the new building as it had in the former building (on the third floor, facing Cameron Street). The work on the building was completed and the dedication ceremonies took place on Washington's birthday.

Plans for the erection of a Masonic Memorial on Shuter's Hill included space to which the old lodge might be moved, partly in replica, partly in original equipment and furnishings. The replica room was dedicated on February 22, 1943, substantially as we see it today.

There is a presence in this hall that seems to come from the unusual pastel portrait centered on the far wall. It is undeniably a portrait of George Washington, but startlingly different from the ones done in oils by Gilbert Stuart, Charles Willson Peale, Rembrandt Peale and others—of the General astride his noble Nelson, of the President formally posed amid the appurtenances of office. Here instead is the likeness of an old man, his strong, deeply lined face showing the strain of long years of public service, his eyes looking directly ahead yet focused on some distant scene, whether past or present, who can say? The tired face shows the scars of smallpox contracted when he was a young man in Barbados with his half-brother, Lawrence, the deep remnant of a wound on the left cheek, a mole beneath the right ear. This is George Washington as his masonic associates knew him in 1793. With his permission they commissioned William Williams of Philadelphia with the instructions: "Paint the President just as he is," wearing the regalia and jewels of a Master Mason. When the portrait was completed, Washington gave his approval and it was hung in the Lodge Room.

Beneath the portrait is a high-back black leather chair which Washington brought up from the library at Mount

Two young visitors pay their respects to the towering bronze statue of Washington in the Memorial Museum.

Vernon when he served as Master of the Lodge. It has occupied center position in the lodge hall ever since; and each
succeeding Master, at his installation, has sat in it.

Arranged against the wall around the room are two small
desks, armed Windsor chairs, a dozen straight chairs with
beautifully contoured seats, an interesting corner bench, three
long benches, two black leather chairs and six plain kitchen-
type chairs, two from Mount Vernon. Of this authentic,
time-polished furniture, every piece with the exception of
four chairs is from the old lodge hall.

Each of the glass cases along the long north and south walls
contains articles of rare value. The identification cards beside
each, with their careful documentation, can give only the
brief facts associated with each museum acquisition, yet each
has its own special story. There is, for instance, the account
of an English Freemason who became desperately sick in
Gadsby's Tavern. Members of the local fraternity saw to it
that he was well cared for until he was able to return home.
He refused to give his name, and the incident was closed until
four years later when 2,500 pieces of the finest cut glass
arrived as a gift to the Masonic lodge, each piece engraved
with the Masonic emblem, the initial and number of the lodge.
Most of the collection has been lost, but a few remaining
pieces substantiate a story worth telling.

Many articles are personally associated with George Washington throughout his life. From his early years there is a
small pen knife, a gift from his mother when he acquiesced
in her objection to his acceptance of an appointment as a
midshipman in the English navy; and there are his pocket
compass and other surveying instruments reminiscent of the
time when, as an apprentice surveyor, he helped lay out the
first streets and lots in Alexandria. As you read about the
articles, events of the past seem to come alive. This is particularly true when you look at the medicine scales and the
bleeding instruments used during Washington's last illness,
and the chamber clock which was in his bedroom at Mount

George Washington, portrait painted about 1783 by Joseph Wright
who, Washington wrote, "is thought to have taken a better likeness
of me than any other painter has done." The portrait is in the
Cleveland Museum of Art, Hinman B. Hurlburt Collection.

Vernon. In accordance with the custom of the time, Dr. Elisha Cullen Dick, one of the three attending physicians, cut the cord of the pendulum thereby stopping the clock forever at 10:20 on the evening of December 14, 1799. The clock was a gift to Washington's lodge, presented by Martha Washington.

One of the Museum treasures is believed to be the only complete set of early English uniform weights and measures in this country. This includes a four-foot rule for measuring lumber, liquid measures for a pint, a quart and a gallon; dry measures for a quarter-peck, half-peck, a peck and a bushel, and standard weights from one pound to twenty-eight pounds. Merchants dealing in such commodities as tobacco, grain, flour, indeed, everything from snuff to yard goods, were required to check their own measures by the uniform standards.

Also enshrined in this great Memorial building is a comparatively new George Washington Museum, dedicated February 22, 1966. It includes a Washington family bible, which was presented a year earlier, and a wealth of Washington memorabilia.

Each year additional treasures come to this safe repository atop a hill in Alexandria. It was known as Shuter's Hill in the years prior to the Civil War, the name coming from a local man who was given land on the hill in exchange for some marshland on which he and his family had been living at a river wharf site. During the Civil War, when Fort Ellsworth was built near the summit and was used for a rifle range, among other services, the soldiers began calling the area Shooter's Hill—a reasonable explanation for two spellings in various histories.

A recent addition in the Masonic Memorial is a medallion honoring President Gerald Ford, himself a member of the Masonic order.

4 Alexandria Digs up its Past

Note: Under the direction of a City Archeological Commission, City Archeologist Richard Muzzrole and his staff, the rescue activities described in this section are part of an expanding and continuing program. Visitors may discover the archeologist and his assistants, including volunteers from nearby colleges and high schools, at work behind any white board fence enclosing a recently-cleared area in the old port section.

Arrangements may be made to visit the Archeological Laboratory to watch such restoration work as may be in progress. This is a type of historic reclamation that is rarely observable on site. The program is being followed with interest by many old towns in other parts of the country and by curators of museums in the United States and England.

For information about the work that may be in progress at a specific time, telephone the Archeological Laboratory, 683-2062, or write: Chairman, Archeological Commission, City Hall, Alexandria, Va. 22313.

The photographs in this section are used by permission of Richard Muzzrole, City Archeologist, the Alexandria Archeological Commission and the Smithsonian Institution.

ARTIFACT DISPLAYS
AND ON SITE DIGGINGS

A STOCKY, well-muscled Boston-bred "rescue archeologist" began in 1965 to make Alexandria the envy of every old city in America interested in acquiring more of its artifactual history. One authority goes far enough to say, "Alexandria is sitting upon the Mother Lode of Americana."

Exhibits of the city's newly-restored treasures in porcelain, pottery, glass and other articles of interest and value that were broken, discarded, buried and forgot for at least 150 years now fill display cases in the lobby of City Hall, Ramsay House, and the exhibition building at Gunston Hall. They form a dramatic picture-book of the past that needs little reading matter.

Scientists at Colonial Williamsburg, the Corning Glass Works, Winterthur, Michigan's Ford Museum and the Staffordshire Museum at Stoke-on-Trent, England, are among those alert for the cultural information that the Alexandria excavations may disclose.

The man who is almost entirely responsible for this achievement did not arrive in the old port city as did many of its early settlers—by boat at the waterfront. He came prosaically

177

Rescue Archeologist Richard Muzzrole, just up from exploring a privy well.

and informally by bus from Washington one day with town map in hand and trowel in pocket. There was no fanfare, no welcoming committee; but there were plan and purpose behind his visit.

The City of Alexandria had committed itself to a greatly needed Urban Renewal program which necessitated the razing of some deteriorating and generally undistinguished store buildings. These were located in the block designated as Market Square, bounded by King, Fairfax and Royal streets, the area where a fountain now plays and band concerts are held on summer evenings. This was a part of oldest Alexandria; but the buildings that were being demolished were not the first to be erected on the property. Here, for most of two hundred years buildings had come and gone, victims of expansion, of fire, of time. The great old buildings still standing that represented so vital a part of the city's past had been excluded from the renewal program, each to be maintained and, when required, to be restored.

People had lived and worked in this area during the early years when such municipal facilities as running water, sewer connections, indoor plumbing and paved streets were dreams yet to be realized. Wells and privies and stepping-stones and town pumps provided the necessary accommodations of the times for town-dwellers here as elsewhere. Nearly unbelievable is the fact that only one interior bathroom in colonial America has been documented. It was at Whitehall, the estate of Governor Horatio Sharpe, near Annapolis, Maryland. Housed at the end of an arcade from a bedroom, in a small semi-octagonal building topped by a Chippendale railing, there were two toilet bowls, each cut from a solid block of marble and fed by rainwater caught in a rooftop cistern which was discharged into a cesspool.

Alexandria had its own unique facilities. These were privy wells, constructed in a way that has not been discovered elsewhere. Sunk like wells, they are approximately five feet in diameter and are expertly lined with bricks, dry-laid in stretchers, to an average depth of 25 feet, sometimes 30 feet. Some of these privies—and during the course of recent exploration scores of them have been located and investigated—had rim supports indicating, as old insurance records verify, that they formed the sturdy foundation for two-story brick "necessary" structures. Almost without exception these privies served a secondary purpose: as convenient depositories for the things people throw away. While much that was discarded in the late eighteenth and early nineteenth centuries, as today, really *was* trash and much that undoubtedly would have historic interest and value has been composted by time and the elements, such materials as china, pottery, glass, metals, wood and leather have survived.

When the first urban renewal area had been cleared of buildings, debris and foundations, and then leveled according to contract, some highly-interesting core borings suggested that these long abandoned and long-buried reservoirs of a past culture might be worth investigating. Would the Smithsonian Institution be interested?

The fact is accepted by all archeologists that in an excavating project, whether in ancient Greece, Egypt, Israel or Alexandria, Virginia, the privies are a prime source of artifacts. So the answer to the official city inquiry was the arrival of a museum technician named Richard Muzzrole, with instructions from the prestigious repository of the nation's past to dig in. That is why he brought the trowel.

All the privy wells in Alexandria were dug during a 60 year period between 1749–52 and 1810. In May of the latter year, a sanitation conscious common council ordered that no more such wells could be sunk and that within ten years all must be filled in, under the direction of the superintendent of police. The old ordinance still stands on the record, but the truth is that compliance and enforcement were both casual and delayed. Much material of architectural value was deposited after the end of the grace period.

The essence of archeology is to dig *in a meaningful way* so

that what is being done tells a story. Thus, the first step, after locating a privy well, is to remove the material with which it was filled: dirt, ashes, oyster shells, anything that came to hand. Each of these deep wells is, in a sense, a time capsule in which the past of a family, a workshop, an inn, indeed, of a town, is stored layer upon layer upon layer, down into the subsoil.

The work of opening one such time capsule began two doors south of Gadsby's Tavern. The fill material was removed, then the most recently discarded of the artifacts. The first physical proof of the importance of the project was revealed when these bucketsful of artifacts were taken to Smithsonian Institution for evaluation. Thereafter, with growing confidence, working deeper each day in black and unsavory muck and mire, beneath a shrinking halo of sky, the rescue archeologist was rewarded with the excitement of rare discoveries. These were, superficially, filthy, time-encrusted bits and pieces of china, pottery, glass, too stained almost to be recognizable, mixed in with spectacle cases, leather shoes, broken-toothed tortoise shell combs, bent spoons, children's toys. To the trained eye, they were recognizable parts of a puzzle which, when properly cleaned, assembled and fitted together would increase the knowledge of early life in Alexandria.

The work is hard and demanding. It requires not only the physical labor of bringing up basketsful or bucketsful of material to the surface, but the on-site labeling of each container: the location and number of the privy well from which it has come, the date of the find, and the exact strata in the well from which the haul has been made. Notebook after notebook was filled with the hieroglyphics of the profession. Without this exacting documentation, the value of the digging is substantially minimized. This fact explains in part the caution given to amateur enthusiasts in private sectors of the old town who would explore their own gardens as a first self-taught lesson in archeology.

From deep in a well, the worker sees only a small area of sky.

Each layer, going down to the bottom of a well is older than the one above it only as to the *time* at which a deposit was made. A box of glass arriving from England and broken in transit might be thrown into a privy well along with a broken treasure many generations older. Only the artifacts themselves can serve to identify the time and place of their manufacture. Rare treasures can, therefore, be expected at any level.

The work is admittedly dirty and laborious. It is done in narrow, cramped quarters and awkward positions, without benefit of cross-ventilation. The possibility of a cave-in or the dislodging of stones is always in mind; but the digging is only the preliminary part of a complete rescue operation. The next step, after the on-site documentation, is taken in the laboratory. There, everything that has been recovered must first be carefully cleaned. A thorough soaking and washing may suffice for such artifacts as china, pottery and glass. The shards begin to show color, patterns and designs that suggest the whole article to which so many fragments belong. The delicate handle of a rare old china cup almost cries out for reunion with the body of the cup from which it was long ago broken. Large fragments of a choice pottery tureen seem to magnetize the smaller bits that belong to it.

Articles of metal, including silver and pewter, leather and wood, perhaps some long-gone grandfather's favorite gold-headed cane, require long and tedious baths in various chemicals as the beginning of their restoration. After the cleaning, everything must be separated, labeled and placed in shallow boxes: pottery here, china fragments there, bits and pieces of glass in another. Years may be required before the major part of the material can be properly reconstructed for display.

The digging did, indeed, begin quietly in the first of the privy wells, but scarcely inconspicuously. It was done, as it still is being done, in full sight of passers-by, many of them curious. Some stopped to look, some hung around the top of a well to watch and ask questions; a choice few wanted to help.

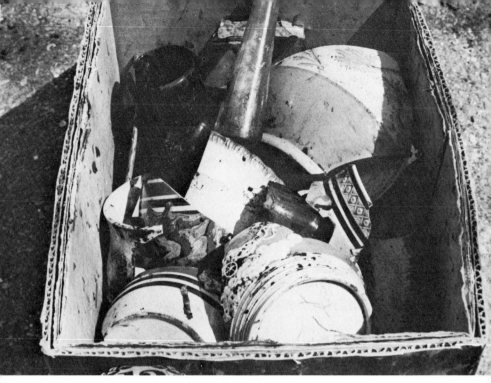

Artifacts as they are brought to the surface.

In short time a leading city lawyer was up to his boots in the mud, camera in hand, making an invaluable pictorial record of the work. Several firemen volunteered for off-duty assistance and helpful suggestions. Young people were interested, too, eager to learn—and some of those who watched the "mess and gunk" that seemed to be so important as it was brought to the surface came along into the laboratory to find out why. The laboratory scarcely deserved the name at first. It was a makeshift work place set up in borrowed space not far from the digging. It would be expanded into an efficient, well-organized laboratory where interested spectators can now learn how rescue archeology is achieved.

After some 25 privy wells in the block on which building construction was about to begin had been located and 18 explored, Smithsonian Institution authorities expressed the opinion that the rescue project had served its purpose. Five years of work had been done. The exploration of other wells, although a meager fifteen percent of those known to exist in the block had been investigated thoroughly, would provide no more than " a repetitive and redundant" yield of artifacts. The story of the Alexandria privy wells had been adequately told.

But the story had only begun to be told.

During the summer of 1971 despair and determination were in a tug-of-war as time hurried on and the bulldozers moved relentlessly but necessarily into the areas where shabby buildings had been sacrificed to the requirements of urban development.

The rescue archeologist was unalterably committed to the opinion that the ultimate value of the project he had undertaken and pursued to this point lay more in what he might yet dig up than in the discoveries already made. Not one precious day's work could be lost in negotiations. Once building had begun on the site, the wells and their contents would be sealed forever. He would continue on the job, using his severance pay so far as it would stretch. He still had tenuous hold on work space in a vast warehouse-type building, the Torpedo Plant of "temporary" World War I and World War II construction on the Alexandria waterfront. It was a gloomy place where he shared quarters with the skeletons of prehistoric mammoths from the Smithsonian and the awesome shadows they cast on the grey walls.

The reasons for his opinion were sound. The town of Alexandria which, in years immediately after its founding was almost wholly dependent upon England for manufactured goods, early began attracting a variety of craftsmen and artisans to meet local needs. In a letter to Thomas Jefferson, Washington wrote, "A desire of encouraging whatever is useful and economical seems now generally to prevail." Alongside the merchandising shops surrounding Market Square and extending into the adjacent streets, there came the "smith shops" as they are termed in the records: silversmiths, potters,

Laboratory work consumes much
of Muzzrole's time.

cabinet makers, harness makers, glass makers and all the rest, justly proud of their wares, as surviving examples show they well should have been. A number of these shops were located in the 300 block of King Street which was swept by a devastating fire in 1827. The blaze originated in the workshop of James Green, a cabinet maker of ability and talent whose furniture is currently being studied with interest. Aided by a strong wind, the flames were quickly out of control, racing toward Fairfax Street and the riverfront. The rear portions, particularly, of dwellings and stores fronting on King and Fairfax streets and running from the alley where Green's workshop was located were badly damaged—57 buildings in all.

One of the buildings suffering fire damage was that of Joseph Ingle, another cabinet maker. It was he who, in 1799, made the handsome mahogany coffin for George Washington, complete with lining, lace, and engraved silver plate, for $88.

Another shop damaged was that of John Adam, silversmith, at 318 King Street. Among the artifacts rescued from this area alone, such as the crucibles in which gold and silver were melted, is much that enables a reconstruction of the block historically, beyond the documentation of deeds and records.

By November, 1973, city officials were sufficiently convinced as to the importance of continuing the project to place the rescue archaeologist on the city payroll under the supervision of the City Manager's office. The exploration of the privy wells in the 400 block of King Street, again working against time, was assured. With such volunteer assistance as was available, it was quickly under way.

Confidence in the on-going value of the digs in this block to yield far more than "repetitive finds" began to be substantiated in short time. From a privy well located behind the original plant of the Alexandria *Gazette* came ten pounds of eighteenth century type which, records confirmed, had been discarded in 1815. At that time, new type was proudly announced and used by the paper. Exhaustive examination of this material over a period of months at Smithsonian Institution indicates that the find is one of no more than three or four comparable discoveries in the country and, from the point of view of typographical experts, possibly the most significant.

Another and even more exciting discovery came with the location behind a building in the 200 block of South Washington Street of the waster pile of Alexandria's undisputed master potter. From this one well alone about three feet of solid pottery shards were recovered.

The potter was Henry Piercy, of German descent, from Philadelphia. He served under Washington through most of the Revolutionary War. Tradition in the Piercy family is that a brother, Christian, had a workshop at Valley Forge where he made pots for the soldiers encamped there. Christian Piercy's daughter, Catherine, married Captain John McKnight, ship master and for some years harbor-master of the port of Alexandria. Henry Piercy may well have been influenced directly by Washington to settle in Alexandria. He arrived in 1792, setting up his kiln and workshop at the northeast corner of Washington and Duke streets. Fairly recently part of an old kiln was unearthed there, but was discarded and lost before its archeological value was recognized. By the end of the year, when Piercy announced the opening of his Earthenware Manufactory he had become a member of the Independent Blues, which he had the honor of commanding at Washington's funeral, and was taking an important part in the life of the town.

The Alexandria area was discovered to be rich in an excellent quality of kaolin, as it still is, suitable for producing a high-grade of pottery. Piercy used this clay to make a lead-glazed earthenware in all the shapes and for all the purposes his customers and the times required. Examples of his pottery have been found at Mount Vernon as well as in Alexandria.

In addition to his pottery manufactory, Piercy also maintained for a time a retail crockery shop in the 400 block of King Street. Here he sold not only his own wares but the finest

A restored bowl is a thing of beauty.

of imported china. Other potters were also taking advantage of both the good clay and the good market in Alexandria. Among the best known were Thomas Fisher, James Miller, Thomas Hughes, Lewis Plum, John Swann and Benedict Milburn.

By the time the Piercy waster pile material was examined, the rescue archeologist was so familiar with the individual characteristics of each potter that he could pick up a shard, examine it closely, and say definitely, "This is Piercy. See . . ." Today thousands of these shards are housed in the archeological laboratory awaiting assembly and restoration. Others have been restored wholly or in substantial part and are on display there. Among the many beautiful china articles—cups and bowls and tureens and platters—is an English creamware bowl, dated 1785, that came from the well behind the tavern operated by Richard Arell. It is decorated in polychrome colors over glaze, with a large red rose—"the King's rose"—on the outside. Beneath a narrow pink border on the inside of the bowl is this inscription:

> *"Thus happy with my bowl and friend,*
> *May I in pleasure every evening spend."*

As the archeological program continues into the 500 block, there will be many such excellent examples of eighteenth and early nineteenth century china, pottery and glass available for display throughout the city and in waiting museums. In addition to the large collection of glass that has been recovered from local glassmakers, and is currently being prepared for display, there is always the possibility that important new discoveries may be made. Some of the private residences and leading hostelries of colonial and early federal Alexandria were well-furnished with the best table services the times produced. Shards taken from privy wells behind the residence, for instance, of Samuel Snowden, or McKnight's Tavern could, today, set a table with china and glass of museum quality. Two particularly fine tankards and the shards of at least three others are believed to be most certainly the work of Henry William Stiegel, whose glass houses were in Pennsylvania. It may well be that glass articles made by Caspar Wistar, in Salem County, New Jersey, and John Frederick Amelung, nearby in Frederick, Maryland, are yet to be discovered. The products of Amelung were well-known in Alexandria, as represented by two large goblets engraved with the Washington coat-of-arms which Amelung presented to the President in 1789.

In 1975 the City of Alexandria established an Archeological Commission charged with the responsibilities:

> *To establish goals and priorities with a view to excavating, preserving, and restoring and displaying the artifacts which contribute to the history and heritage of colonial, federal and historic Alexandria, historic Virginia and historic America.*

Ten years had passed since a rescue archeologist arrived by

bus in Alexandria with a trowel in his pocket. With it, he laid the foundation for an archeological program of tremendous value and lasting importance.

All recovered material, including that collected while the Smithsonian Institution sponsored the project, is and will remain the property of the City of Alexandria.

The archeological program embraces other projects in addition to the excavation of the privy wells. Every old town contains a wealth of buried treasure in many forms: the foundations of long-gone buildings, perhaps Indian artifacts, certainly in a river port town such as Alexandria remnants of wharves and ships. Alexandria is keenly alert to the possibilities, and has instructed the Archeological Commission to investigate and list possible sites and, through cooperation with nearby schools and colleges, to develop courses in archeology for students.

It is an on-going program well worth watching.

5 Remnants of the Ramparts

THE EARLIEST RAMPARTS

THE earliest bastion of defense in what is now Alexandria, according to some interesting old histories—and no two give exactly the same account—may have been a fort for protection against Indians. Certainly the Indians in the area, particularly those of the Dogue tribe, had become more than troublesome neighbors to the first hardy traders and settlers who ventured into their historic territory.

Was John Carlyle's handsome mansion built in 1752 upon the foundations of such a fort? Some legends claim that it was. No known documents give proof; however, a descent alone into the cold, deep, musty darkness of the dungeon-like rock-walled cellar rooms, before the house was closed for restoration, could conjure ghosts to match all the old tales.

THE SEA WALL

Another rampart was erected against the infrequent rampages of an ordinarily friendly and placid Potomac River. This was a sea wall, some sections of which still exist, with more sections, perhaps, yet to be uncovered.

Guns on the Northwest Bastion
of Fort Ward Park.

Courtesy the curator, Fort Ward Park.

All the early maps of Alexandria show the town located in a cove of the river, between West's Point, at the foot of Oronoco Street, where the first wharves and warehouses were located and from which the first ferry ran across river to Maryland, and Point Lumley, at the foot of Duke Street. While these two points are no longer so prominently like the tips of a new moon holding the small settlement within its curve, they are worth visiting for those interested in the changing shape of the waterfront. The two blocks of Water Street (now Lee Street) between King and Queen Street were at the apex of the curve, and directly on the river. Some of the houses along Fairfax Street had gardens that extended down to the water's edge where the fishing was good. Gradually the river was pushed back by land fills to provide building space for wharves, warehouses and other shipping facilities. Water Street was opened from King to Queen and in time, Union Street was opened, giving access to river front commerce on its east side.

A vantage point from which visitors may see the relationship between the old residences on South Lee Street and the reclaimed land is in Potomac Court. This is entered from Wilkes Street, on the right side, walking eastward from South Lee. The large three-and-a-half story brick house in the 400 block was the home of General Daniel Roberdeau, a French Huguenot, who was prominently active in Philadelphia, served during the Revolutionary War, and came to Alexandria about 1784, probably because of his friendship with Washington. From the front, on South Lee Street, visitors will note its Georgian architecture, the stone trim, and an enormous French lock on the front door which is reportedly much older than the house. From the rear, above Potomac Court, there is a heavy retaining wall with an interesting vine-covered iron gate beneath a lintel which supports an iron fence. It was through this small gate, down steep steps and a path that the General's retinue of servants reached the lower level where their brick quarters were located. These have now been converted into modern residences. The small buildings, three in a row, with their beautifully dentiled brick cornices, indicate the well-planned construction that went into the building of the great house, also.

Alexandria is located well below the fall line of the Potomac River which, here, is subject to the rise and fall of the tides in Chesapeake Bay. Occasionally an exceptionally low tide seems to suck the water from the river, leaving mud flats and revealing the remains of wharves, perhaps an old cannon or the bones of a ship.

Remnants of the sea wall are evident behind the 1757 house at 224 South Lee Street, built by George Johnston, a brilliant lawyer and member of the Virginia House of Burgesses.

Recently other remnants of the sea wall were discovered in the foundation of a house in the 100 block of Prince Street. There is every reason to expect that in a city as archeologically conscious of every aspect of its physical history as is Alexandria new evidences of the sea wall and other remnants of ramparts may be discovered.

JONES POINT LIGHTHOUSE

Drive or hike to the end of South Lee Street (nine blocks from King Street), then turn left and first right under the high approach to Woodrow Wilson Bridge · Parking area · Walk along a firmly-packed gravel road to the bank of the river.

A lighthouse guarding the approach by water to a port town is another form of rampart. Although the Jones Point Lighthouse is not high or impressive in appearance, it is believed to be the oldest inland lighthouse in the United States. The thumb of land dipping into the Potomac River on which the white frame building stands is historic in itself on two counts: it is the southern boundary of the tract of land granted to Margaret Brent in 1654 on which Old Alexandria is located; and it is the point selected by George Washington in 1791 to mark the southern boundary of the first District of Columbia.

A visit to this area today is also important because its strategic position gives you the opportunity of really seeing the broad magnificence of the Potomac River which George Washington described as "one of the finest rivers in the world." It is a pleasant place for a picnic, too, and for rambling along the river bank in search of the historic markers sometimes nearly hidden among the trees. In the center of town glimpses of the river are framed at the foot of such streets as King and Prince by buildings that serve as blinders. The panoramic view from Jones Point emphasizes dramatically the importance to early colonial development of having a port here.

The lighthouse offered both a welcome and a warning. Captains and pilots of ships from all the ports of the eighteenth century world, approaching for the first time the wharves along the Alexandria waterfront, noted its position on river charts and watched for its beacon. To sea captains on the final stage of a long voyage away from home it gave assurance of safe harbor just around the bend.

The lighthouse is closed at present, under the protective custody of the National Park Service until such time as it can be properly restored and the area developed as a part of the Park system.

ON THE ALEXANDRIA WATERFRONT IN WARTIME

During the Revolutionary War and the War of 1812, there were no protecting ramparts along the Alexandria waterfront, yet the enemy thrust was entirely by water. Fortunately, it was not damaging. British vessels were in the Potomac during the Revolution, giving grave concern to George Washington and George Mason, among others whose plantations were vulnerable to attack.

On the morning of Monday, August 29, 1814, Alexandrians awoke to find that during the night, the British frigates *Seahorse* and *Euryalus* had edged up to the wharf during the night, their guns pointing ominously up King Street. Had James Madison and Thomas Jefferson succeeded in winning approval of President Washington and the Congress to build the Capitol of the United States on Shuter's Hill, where the George Washington National Masonic Memorial now rises, the fate of old Alexandria might have been determined on that day. As it was, five days earlier, the British under General Ross, had captured Washington. The frigates sailed away and Alexandria was left unharmed.

During the early months of 1861 war clouds were once more gathering over Washington; however, while seven Southern states had voted to secede from the Union, beginning with South Carolina in January, and the Confederacy had been set up in February, Virginia and North Carolina served as buffer states. On April 17, the Virginia Convention voted secession, subject to a vote by the people on May 23. News came north from Richmond on the evening of that day that secession of Virginia had gone into effect. This was the signal for history-making decisions.

In his white-columned mansion at Arlington and in the homes of friends and relatives on North Washington Street in Alexandria Robert E. Lee had made his personal decision: he was a Virginian and would go with his state. In Washington, President Lincoln's immediate concern was for the Capital. He gave orders that troops should move across the river to occupy Alexandria.

These came in three columns by three routes: one group crossed the river by way of the Long Bridge, approximately the location of the present Fourteenth Street bridge. Another group moved across the so-called Aqueduct Bridge from Georgetown. This was not really a bridge, but the dry bed of an old aqueduct. The third contingent came by boat to the foot of King Street. This was a regiment of New York Fire

Fighters known as the Zouaves, under the command of Colonel Elmer Ellsworth, a colorful and popular leader. Alone, he dashed into the Marshall House, a well-known tavern on King Street, and ripped down the large Confederate flag, proudly catching the early morning spring breeze off the river. He was instantly shot dead by the owner.

THE CIVIL WAR FORTS

Before the day was over, work was begun on a fort located on the crest of Shuter's Hill, with a commanding view of Washington, the Maryland shore and the Potomac River as well as the port of Alexandria. It was given the name Fort Ellsworth. All that remains of this rampart today can be seen best from the top of the George Washington Masonic Memorial—the outline etched in a darker shade of green on the grassy area that covers the old moat and breastworks. As recently as sixty years ago, the fort was reported to be in "perfect state of preservation" and there was some interest in restoring it and developing a park on the hill.

After the battle of Manassas in the autumn of 1861, a circle of forts was built around Washington. The number was increased to 68 forts and batteries before the war was over. Of these ramparts, only three have been restored to any extent. One is Fort Stevens, in Washington, where President Lincoln watched General Jubal Early in action. While many presidents of the United States have served in the Armed Forces and have been under combat fire, this is the only instance in which a president, while in office, witnessed a battle at close range. The other two forts are Marcy, on the George Washington Memorial Parkway, and Fort Ward, fifth largest in the chain and the most interesting one to Alexandrians.

FORT WARD PARK
4301 West Braddock Road

Museum—Open daily 9:00 a.m. to 5:00 p.m. · Open Sundays— noon to 5:00 p.m. · Closed Thanksgiving & Christmas · No admission charge.

Park—Open daily 9:00 a.m. to sunset.

Part of an old cannon mounted on a foundation of cobble- stones removed long ago from downtown streets stands at the intersection of Braddock Road and Russell Road in a newer residential section of Alexandria. As the marble tablet indicates, the cannon points up the hill over which the English General Edward Braddock led his red-coated regulars and a contingent of the Virginia militia into the "western wilderness" during the French and Indian War in 1755.

The hill was steep, the road rough, the pace labored for the horses struggling to pull the General in a chariot which he had borrowed from Governor Sharpe, of Maryland; straining against the heavy military equipment and the heavily loaded wagons of supplies. For many young Alexandrians belonging to the Virginia militia who had trained with so much enthusiasm in Market Square, their last view of home would be from this hill. Weeks after their departure, Braddock's forces were ambushed on the banks of the Monongahela deep in the mountains. The death toll was high, including General Braddock and many of the local young men.

Braddock Road, easily traveled today, was again the troop route when, in May of 1861, President Lincoln ordered the hasty erection of Fort Ward at the top of the hill. Today, this historic landmark is a 40-acre woodland park surrounding the Fort. The City of Alexandria, which has owned the park since 1964, has spent over a half-million dollars on its development. The Northwest Bastion has been carefully restored. Here are mounted six guns, exact replicas of the 36 placed in the Fort during the Civil War. There are also a bomb shelter and pow-

der magazine. Much of the old ditch that ran around the Fort can be easily explored as can the many miles of trenches. A museum and Officers' Hut were reconstructed from photographs of wartime buildings in Alexandria. Today the park provides seven well-equipped picnic areas, rest quarters and an amphitheater where concerts are given regularly on Thursday evenings throughout the summer as well as many special performances.

The purpose of a rampart is to protect. Fort Ward was such a rampart. It was never under attack, its guns never went into action, no blood was shed here.

Ramparts are not always constructed of stone and mortar, are not always physical structures where guns are mounted and soldiers keep watch. Such ramparts as these cannot in time become woodland parks where picnics are spread and children play. These are the intangible ramparts of democracy—the priceless heritage of freedom over which alert Americans must stand eternal guard. Here in Alexandria and Northern Virginia more than two centuries ago a small group of remarkably gifted men with a high sense of human values and an illuminating perspective had a leading part in originating, planning, articulating and implementing the laws guaranteeing our freedom. In a very real sense these are the ramparts we watch through all the long nights of time, to be sure that with each day in tomorrow's history as the morning fog lifts from the river, here and everywhere our flag, wherever it is raised, is a symbol of freedom as it flies strong and flies free.

President Gerald Ford continues to own the home in Alexandria in which he and his family lived throughout his service in the Congress of the United States.
The 38th President, like the first President, participated in many activities in the town. Here, he speaks in front of the Friendship Fire Engine Company house.

Photograph by Star-News Photographer Paul M. Schmick, used by permission curator of the Fire House museum.

USEFUL INFORMATION FOR VISITORS

For information about: *Inquire at:*

Free parking permits for
  out of town visitors
Lists of restaurants in Old Town   Alexandria Tourist Council
Lists of specialty shops   Headquarters
  in Old Town   221 King Street
Free maps of Old Alexandria   Open daily 9:30 a.m. to 4:30 p.m.
Location of churches
Motels   Telephone: 549-0205
Swimming pools
Tour guides (local)
Special events   and
Sightseeing Tours (bus)
Boat trips on Potomac
Playgrounds   Bicentennial Headquarters
Mount Vernon   201 South Washington Street
Gunston Hall   Open seven days a week
Woodlawn Plantation and other   9 a.m. to 5 p.m.
  places of interest near Alexandria
Bicentennial Events in Virginia   Telephone: 548-1776
Travel
Motels

Important Numbers

Alexandria Hotline (24 hour service):
an emergency referral service that
covers 800 public and private agencies 548-3810

American Automobile Association
Alexandria Office
312 South Washington Street 549-1080

Police Department 750-6411

Ambulance-rescue service
Fire Department 549-5100

Alexandria City Hospital
Emergency Department
4320 Seminary Road 370-9000

Poison Control Center 370-9000

Public Library
717 Queen Street 750-6351

Recreation Department 750-6325

American Red Cross
Alexandria Office
401 Duke Street 549-8300

Weather 936-1212

BIBLIOGRAPHY

A Hornbook of Virginia History. Richmond: Virginia State Library, 1965.

Alexandria. Compiled by W. P. A. Archives Dept. U.S. Government, 1939.

Alexandria, A Composite History, Vol. 1. Edited by Elizabeth Hamble-ton & Marian Van Landingham. Alexandria Bicentennial Commission publication, 1975.

Alexandria, U.S.A. Yesteryears Remembered. Alexandria: Pub. by First & Citizens National Bank, 1964.

Biographical Memoirs of the Illustrious Gen. George Washington, comp. Barnard, Vt. Joseph Dix, 1813.

BROCKETT, F. L. *The Lodge of Washington, 1783–1876.* Alexandria, 1890.

BROWN, William A. *The History of Royal Arch Masonry in Alexandria, Virginia.* Baltimore: Saratoga Printing & Lithographing Co.

BROWN, Stuart E. *Virginia Baron.* Berryville, Va. Chesapeake Book Co., 1965.

BRUCE, Philip Alexander. *Economic History of Virginia in the 17th Century.* New York: MacMillan & Co., 1896. (2 vols.)

CALLAHAN, Charles H. *Washington: The Man and the Mason.* George Washington National Memorial Association, 1913.

CATON, James R. *Legislative Chronicle of the City of Alexandria.* Alexandria: Newell-Cole, 1933.

CHAPMAN, Sigismunda Mary Frances. *History of the Chapman and Alexander Families.* Richmond: Dietz Press, 1946.

DAVIS, Deering, Stephen P. Dorsey and Ralph Cole Hall. *Alexandria Houses. 1750–1830.* New York: Bonanza Books, 1946.

Files of Alexandria Gazette, in microfilm, Alexandria Library.

FLEMING, Thomas J. *First in their Hearts.* New York: W. W. Norton & Co., 1967.

GOTTMAN, Jean. *Virginia in Our Century*. Charlottesville: University Press of Virginia, 1969.

GRIMSHAW, William. *History of the United States*. Philadelphia: Grigg & Elliot, 1841.

HENING, William Waller, comp. *The Statutes at Large Being a Collection of All the Laws of Virginia, from the First Session of the Legislature in the Year 1619*. Richmond: 1810–23 (13 vols.).
Laws of Virginia, supplement 1700–1750, 1971.

IRVING, Washington. *Life of Washington*. New York: G. P. Putnam & Co., 1855–56, (4 vols.).

JACKSON, Eugene B. *The Romance of Historic Alexandria*. Alexandria: Harry W. Wade, Pub 1923.

Journal of William Loughton Smith. Boston: Massachusetts Historical Society *Proceedings* October 1917-June 1918.

HALLOWELL, Benjamin. *Autobiography*. Philadelphia, 1883.

Homes and Gardens in Old Virginia. Garden Club of Virginia, 1930.

KABLER, Dorothy H. *The Story of Gadsby's Tavern*. Alexandria: Newell-Cole, 1952.

LANCASTER, Robert A., Jr. *Historic Virginia Homes and Churches*. New York: J. B. Lippincott, 1915.

LEE, Edmund Jennings. *Lee of Virginia*. Philadelphia, 1895.

LINDSEY, Mary. *Historic Homes and Landmarks of Alexandria, Virginia*. Alexandria: The Landmarks Society, 14th printing, 1974.

MCGROARTY, William Buckner. *The Old Presbyterian Meeting House at Alexandria, Va. 1774–1874*. Richmond: William Byrd Pres 1940.

MOORE, Gay Montague. *Seaport in Virginia*. Richmond: Garrett and Massie, 1949.

Mount Vernon: A Handbook. The Mount Vernon Ladies Association of the Union. Washington: Judd & Detweiler, Inc., 1960.

MORRISON, Charles. *The Fairfax Line*. Parsons, W. Va.: McClain Printing Co., 1970.

One Hundred Fifty Years for Christ, comp. History of St. Mary's Roman Catholic Church (Souvenir edition).

Our Town 1749–1865. Pub. by Alexandria Association, 1956.

POWELL, Mary G. *The History of Old Alexandria, Va*. Richmond: William Byrd Press, 1928.

REPS, John W. *Tidewater Towns—City Planning in Colonial Virginia and Maryland*. Colonial Williamsburg Foundation, 1972.

SENGEL, William Randolph. *Can these Bones Live?*

SMOOT, Betty Carter (McGuire). *Day in an Old Town*. Privately printed, Alexandria, Va., 1934.

SOMERVILLE, Mollie. *Washington Walked Here*. Washington: Acropolis Books, 1970.

STEWART, George R. *Names on the Land*. New York: Random House, 1945.

STUKENBROEKER, Fern C. *A Watermelon for God*. Alexandria: 1974.

SWEM, Earl G. *Virginia Historical Index*. Roanoke: Stone Printing & Mfg. Co., 1934–36 (2 vols.)

The Charter and Laws of the City of Alexandria, Va., and Historical Sketch of Its Government. Published by the City Council, Alexanderia, Va., 1874.

Unpublished manuscripts, letters and documents, Alexandria Library.

Virginia—The Old Dominion in Pictures. Virginia State Chamber of Commerce. New York: Fleming Pub. Co., 1941.

WASHINGTON, George. *President Washington's Diaries*. Library Edition. Comp. Joseph A. Hoskins. Summerfield, N.C. 1921.

WAYLAND, John W. *Historic Houses of Northern Virginia*. Staunton, Va. McClure Publ. Co., 1937.

WEDDERBURN, Alexander J. *Historic Alexandria, Past and Present*. Souvenir of the Virginia Tercentennial, 1907.

WILLS, deeds and other records. Alexandria City Hall.

Yearbook of the Alexandria Association, 1957.

ABOUT THE AUTHOR

NETTIE ALLEN VOGES was born to write about Old Alexandria. Although she is not a native, her family roots go back to 1654 when a 700-acre tract on which the oldest part of the town now stands was granted to an English spinster, Margaret Brent. Through generations of descendants of Margaret Brent's brother, the story of this intrepid woman became a part of Nettie Allen's heritage. When her marriage brought her to the Washington area it seemed only natural that she and her husband would settle in nearby Alexandria. She has lived there since 1947.

Life and a career in writing began for her in Winston-Salem, North Carolina, where she lived in two eighteenth century houses in the center of the Moravian community of Salem. After being graduated from Salem College and Columbia University School of Journalism, New York, she received a contract for a series of newspaper articles for the Charlotte *Observer* entitled "Trailing George Washington through North Carolina on his Presidential Tour of the South, 1791." The vicissitudes of that trip made fast friends of the first President and the novice journalist, a friendship that has come to full flower in this book about Alexandria, Washington's home town.

During the late 1930s and early 1940s Nettie Allen combined a full time public relations job in Winston-Salem with part time editing of a magazine for young people in Washington, syndicating magazine articles through the educational and religious press, and writing the script for a radio program. Though she sincerely prefers anonymity, she does admit to having written innumerable political speeches and magazine articles and several books. Involvement comes as naturally to her as breathing and has brought her to the forefront of a variety of historic, cultural and philanthropic organizations. She is a director of the Alexandria Association for Restoration and Preservation and served as its president in 1971–72. She is vice-chairman of the Alexandria Forum, a charter member of the Alexandria Historical Society, and a member of the City of Alexandria Archeological Commission.

Widowed now, Mrs. Voges lives in the northern part of Alexandria in a low, white brick house on a hillside rampant with azaleas, magnolias, crape myrtle and perennially overgrown shrubbery. Why not in an old house? "There will be time for that," she says, "when I find the right one and can give it the loving care and attention an old house deserves."